COLLEGE
ENGLISH
The Basics

Second Edition

Kendall Hunt
publishing company

George J. Searles
Mohawk Valley Community College

www.kendallhunt.com
Send all inquiries to:
4050 Westmark Drive
Dubuque, IA 52004-1840

Copyright © 2016, 2017 by George J. Searles

ISBN 978-1-5249-3453-8

Printed in the United States of America

To Ellis

CONTENTS

INTRODUCTION

We write for a variety of reasons: to express ourselves, to entertain, to exchange information, to persuade. And we do so in various social, academic, and professional contexts. Not surprisingly then, there are many different *genres* (kinds) of writing.

These are all quite different from one another in a great many ways. This is because each has a somewhat different purpose and intended reader. Hence their tone will vary. But there are other important contrasts too. Each is laid out differently on the page or screen, each is organized differently, and each employs certain approaches and strategies unique to that kind of writing. In short, each genre follows its own distinct formula. Over the years, these variations have evolved and become standard practice simply because they have proven to be what works best in each context.

If presented with examples of the various genres, most of us could easily identify which were which, even if we found the reasons behind our choices difficult to fully explain. This is because we're all experienced readers, and have therefore developed certain automatic—because subconscious—understandings and assumptions about each kind of writing. In order to be taken seriously, therefore, a writer must satisfy the reader's expectations. A business letter must look and "feel like" a business letter, a newspaper article must look and "feel like" a newspaper article, and so on. Certainly this is true of the academic essay, the main genre emphasized in college-level English courses. It's structured a certain way and includes a number of long-established features. Accordingly, this textbook—intended for use in first-year writing classes—focuses primarily on the academic essay, discussing several main modes of essay development, along with specialized applications such as essay exams, literary criticism, and research-based essays.

But the book goes beyond this principal emphasis to provide coverage of workplace writing as well, reflecting an ongoing trend in composition textbooks published in recent years. In truth, *College English: The Basics* is not just about the kind of writing done in college; it's more than that, equipping you to write well even after graduation, when you'll be called upon to communicate on the job. Accordingly, there are revision checklists, model documents, and helpful exercises throughout, along with an appendix that identifies key strategies for improving your style and another that reviews the fundamentals of spelling, punctuation, and grammar.

In short, you will learn from this book. But how *much* you learn will depend primarily on your own efforts. You must attend class regularly, pay close attention to your professor's lectures, complete all assignments punctually, practice good time-management, and approach your English class—indeed, *all* your classes—with an enthusiastic, upbeat attitude. As with anything, a positive, goal-directed outlook gets the best results.

Acknowledgments

Shout-outs are in order. This book would not have been possible without the expertise of my publishing team at Kendall Hunt: Acquisitions Representative Melissa Lavenz, Project Coordinator Kim Schmidt, Editorial Assistant Megan Drake, and Cover Designer Jennifer Fensterman. I must also recognize my MVCC colleagues, especially librarian Colleen Kehoe-Robinson. And I would be remiss indeed if I failed to mention my students, from whom I've learned so much over the years. In addition, I salute my lifelong friend Frank Tedeschi and my "basketball buddy" John Lapinski; both provide much-appreciated friendship and encouragement. Most importantly, I thank my sons, Jonathan and Colin, and my wife, Ellis.

PART 1

The Most Basic Basics: Purpose, Audience, and Tone

Unless we're writing in a diary or personal journal, we usually write for one reason: to communicate with someone else. But the *specific* purpose of that communication, along with our relationship to the intended reader, greatly influences how the writing is done.

Our purpose may simply be to express ourselves. Sometimes the purpose is to make a request. Very often, the purpose is to provide information or to persuade, or both. Or perhaps the goal is just to amuse or entertain.

But the manner in which these objectives are pursued—singly or in combination—is determined by our audience. The writer and reader may be well-acquainted or may never have met. They may be equals (co-workers, for example) or not, as in the case of an employer and an employee. They may be in basic agreement about the topic or they may be in disagreement or even in conflict. So the "voice" or tone of the writing can vary greatly, from highly conversational to very formal indeed.

Certainly, awareness of these factors—purpose, audience, and tone—is crucial to good writing. The first part of this book explores these fundamental concerns, presenting an overview of the governing principles involved.

CHAPTER 1

Purpose

LEARNING OBJECTIVES

When you complete this chapter, you will be able to

► Determine your purpose for writing
► Apply the basic principles involved in self-expressive, informative, interrogative, persuasive, and entertaining writing

DETERMINING PURPOSE

The first step in the writing process is to understand that writing is done for a variety of different reasons, so it's crucial to determine your own objective. Ask yourself, "Summarized in one sentence, what am I trying to say and *why* am I saying it?" To answer, you must carefully consider your subject matter, focusing on its most important elements. A helpful strategy is to employ the "Five W's" that journalists use to structure the opening sentences of newspaper stories: Who, What, Where, When, and Why. Just as they do for reporters, the Five W's will help you clarify your thinking and identify the key points in your communication.

For example, a probation officer composes a pre-sentencing report to convince the court to grant probation or impose a jail sentence. The officer may recommend either, and will provide supporting information, but the primary purpose of the report is to persuade. In such a case, the Five W's might function as follows:

WHO   **WHAT**   **WHERE**

Thomas Moran should be denied probation and sentenced to state prison,

WHEN   **WHY**

effective immediately, because he is a repeat offender.

The Five W's are not magic. Any piece of writing would have to go far beyond a simple statement of five basic facts. But identifying those details helps you determine whether you are writing to express yourself, to provide or request information, to persuade, to entertain or—as is often the case—to achieve some combination of these goals. Once you decide on this, then and only then are you ready to move forward. But it's necessary to understand the strategies you can use. Let's consider each in some depth.

SELF-EXPRESSIVE WRITING

The main purpose of this kind of writing is to convey the writer's thoughts, feelings, emotions, attitudes, or opinions. Accordingly, self-expressive writing is nearly always phrased in the grammatical *first person* ("I did this," "I did that") and often provides an account of a lived experience the writer considers significant. Such writing typically includes information of a personal nature, and sometimes that material might be entertaining. But if the writer is attempting to defend or justify a particular belief, the narrative might employ strategies typical of persuasive writing.

Here's an example of self-expressive writing, the body of an e-mail from a student to her friend, complaining about a mutual acquaintance:

> I don't want you to think I'm being too impatient, but I've gotta tell you how upset I am with Alicia. She always says she'll be ready to go out when I get to her apartment, but when I get there she's never ready. She always has a million lame excuses and doesn't even apologize. So then we're late for whatever it is we're going to. Last night it happened again. We were supposed to go to an 8:00 movie at the mall, and we got there fifteen minutes late. If this keeps up I'm not gonna hang with her no more.

Since the student is expressing personal emotions—resentment and annoyance—she uses first-person narration, which is typical of e-mail exchanges (even those that are not essentially self-expressive). Her inclusion of the details about the movie lends credibility to her complaint, providing a concrete example to balance her rather overstated wording elsewhere ("always…never…always…a million"). Of course, her lapses into unconventional spelling ("gotta…gonna"), slang ("hang with"), and an ungrammatical double-negative ("not…no more") reflect the e-mail's conversational nature. But in self-expressive writing composed in response to college assignments, such informalities should not appear.

INFORMATIVE WRITING

The purpose of this kind of writing is simply to provide information desired or needed by the reader. Therefore, informative writing is usually phrased objectively, with emphasis on verifiable facts rather than on opinions or beliefs. It often includes statistics and other such data. Obviously, factual accuracy is crucial in informational writing. But if the writing uses information in an attempt to prove a point or promote a particular point of view, then it has become primarily persuasive rather than informational.

Here's an example of informative writing, taken from the *New York Safe Boating* manual:

> New York State law requires that all boats not exceed a speed of 5 miles per hour when within 100 feet of shore, a raft, a dock, or an anchored or moored boat. The only exception to this is when the boat is taking a skier from shore or landing a skier near the shore. On some specific bodies of water the 5 mph limit has been extended to 200 feet, and on several lakes there are daytime and nighttime speed limits. Local ordinances may further regulate the speed of boats operated within specific areas.

This manual is studied by persons enrolled in the state's comprehensive boating course, which teaches the fundamentals of safe boating operation. Clearly, all the information in the manual is needed by those readers. With its precise identification of the various speed limits and distances, the above paragraph is representative of the manual's contents, and its objective tone and detailed wording are typical of most informative writing.

INTERROGATIVE WRITING

The purpose of this kind of writing is to request information desired or needed by the writer. First-person narration is often used, by way of explaining the writer's reasons for the inquiry. *Specificity* is the key to effective interrogative writing. The writer must ensure that the reader knows exactly what information is required, and in what degree of detail. Therefore, this kind of writing must not be vague or general. Instead, it must precisely "spell out," in all its particulars, what's being asked for and why.

Here's the body of an e-mail written by a newspaper reporter to the local police chief, requesting information about an arrest:

> It is our understanding that an Arlington resident, Mr. Alexander Booth, is the subject of an investigation by your department, with the assistance of the county district attorney. In keeping with the provisions of the state Freedom of Information Law, we're requesting information about Mr. Booth's arrest.
>
> This information is needed to provide our readership with accurate news coverage. *The Weekly News* prides itself on fair, accurate, and objective reporting, and we're counting on your assistance as we seek to uphold those standards.
>
> In particular, we need to know what charges are pending against Mr. Booth, and the sources of those allegations. In addition, we are requesting a dated chronological summary of the events leading to Mr. Booth's present situation.
>
> Because police records are by law a matter of public record, we anticipate your full cooperation.

This e-mail begins by providing some background, explaining the reasons for its request. But it becomes quite pointed in the third paragraph, where it details its exact requirements, just as all interrogative writing should. Notice also that the reporter has chosen first-person *plural* narration, using words like "we" and "our" rather than "I" and "my," thereby conveying a stronger sense of entitlement to the information. This is essentially a persuasive strategy intended to minimize any resistance on the reader's part. Of course, the e-mail clearly establishes the newspaper's right to the information by mentioning the laws governing such matters, but the first-person plural always suggests greater authority. Indeed, in olden times, kings and queens would employ the *royal "we"* when addressing their subjects.

PERSUASIVE WRITING

The purpose of this kind of writing is to convince the reader of something, or to urge the reader to adopt a particular stance toward something about which the reader and the writer already agree. At its most effective, persuasive writing is phrased objectively (like informational writing) rather than using first-person narration. To succeed, persuasive writing must adopt a reasonable tone, perhaps acknowledging opposing viewpoints before asserting its own. But its claims must be supported by solid evidence, not simply emotional appeals. And the writer must be careful not to stumble into other kinds of fallacy (faulty reasoning) as well. Persuasive writing is perhaps the most difficult kind to accomplish successfully, and is covered in depth in Chapter 7.

Here's a brief "letter to the editor," urging readers to vote for a particular mayoral candidate:

> Clearly, Judith Ayres deserves re-election as mayor of Derbyville. Her opponent, John Daly, is also a worthy candidate, but lacks experience and cannot match the mayor's track record. Now completing her first term in office, Ayres has reduced violent crime by 30%. In addition, she has attracted three large new businesses to the town, thereby adding many thousands of dollars to the tax rolls and creating hundreds of new employment opportunities for local residents. Finally, her direct personal involvement has led to the recent opening of the Senior Citizens Center downtown, a project that the previous administration had been talking about for several years without taking any concrete steps to move it forward. In short, Judith Ayres obviously knows how to make things happen. She deserves your vote on election day next week!

Notice that the writer of this letter has created the appearance of objectivity by respectfully mentioning the opposing candidate before moving on to list the preferred candidate's credentials. And those accomplishments provide support for the letter's objective: to persuade readers to re-elect the mayor. Indeed, if this letter were expanded into a conventional college essay, the mayor's three main achievements—described in greater detail—would provide solid, highly persuasive content for the essay's body paragraphs. Notice also that the paragraph—like most persuasive essays—opens and closes with a firm statement of the writer's position.

ENTERTAINING WRITING

Usually the purpose of this kind of writing is to amuse. This is harder than it sounds, partly because today's media-saturated readers are accustomed to being entertained by professional comedians and commentators. To succeed, this kind of writing must make the reader laugh—or at least smile—by using the techniques perfected by the pros. Principal among these is *reversal of expectation*. All humor derives from unanticipated violation of norms, perhaps by comic exaggeration, or by presenting a familiar reality in a new and different light, or by simply poking irreverent fun at a widespread but questionable assumption. But too much humor relies heavily on crude (and often offensive) "cheap shots" that lack depth or sophistication. By contrast, the very best such writing is that which makes us *think* after we've stopped laughing.

This joke is a good example of entertaining writing:

> A police officer is driving her patrol car when she notices a snail lying on the side of the road with its shell cracked and its hat knocked off. She quickly stops the car, jumps out, and runs to the snail's side to offer assistance. "Mr. Snail, what happened?" the officer asks. "Oh, it was terrible," the snail replies. "I was mugged by three turtles!" Taking out her pencil and notebook, the officer asks, "Three turtles. What did they look like?" And the snail moans, "I don't know. It all happened so fast."

In general it's a bit pointless to explain a joke. Either it's funny or not. But in this case we easily identify several basic features of writing that attempts to amuse. Most obviously, snails don't wear hats or get mugged, and they don't talk. Not so immediately apparent about this joke, however, is its underlying truth: the fact that all perception is subjective. To a snail (who literally moves "at a snail's pace") turtles *would* seem fast, even if they appear slow to the rest of us. So the joke is a subtle reminder about the relative nature of reality, and therein lies its deeper appeal.

But a piece of writing does not necessarily have to amuse in order to provide diversion. Sometimes entertainment is more sober in intention, seeking to deal with weightier issues. Indeed, much serious literature—poetry, fiction, drama—illustrates this. In the broadest sense, literature is certainly a form of entertainment. But it does not always make us smile or laugh. At its best, it makes us *think*. Therefore, it can sometimes sadden—maybe even make us weep. This autobiographical poem, by Belgrade-born former United States Poet Laureate Charles Simic, is a good example.

Old Soldier

By the time I was five,
I had fought in hundreds of battles,
Had killed thousands
And suffered many wounds
Only to rise and fight again.

After the bombing raids, the sky was full
Of flying cinders and birds.
My mother took me by the hand
And led me into the garden
Where the cherry trees were in flower.

There was a cat grooming herself
Whose tail I wanted to pull,
But I let her be for a moment,
Since I was busy swinging at flies
With a sword made of cardboard.

All I needed was a horse to ride,
Like the one hitched to a hearse,
Outside a pile of rubble,
Waiting with its head lowered
For them to finish loading the coffins.

Although playful on the surface, Simic's poem addresses very serious concerns, specifically the horrors of war and their negative, desensitizing effects on children. At the same time, it affirms the presence of certain reassuring constants in life: the survival instinct, the attentiveness of mothers, and the enduring resilience of the natural world.

As we have seen, the different kinds of writing—self-expressive, informative, interrogative, persuasive, and entertaining—are not always mutually exclusive, so a given piece of writing can serve two or more overlapping purposes simultaneously. But whether one or more than one purpose is being pursued, each kind possesses certain identifiable characteristics. Therefore, student writers wishing to improve their skills should familiarize themselves with those features, in order to produce writing that achieves its objectives in every kind of situation.

EXERCISES

1. Identify the purpose(s) of each of the following pieces of writing: a) to self-express; b) to provide information; c) to seek information; d) to persuade; or e) to entertain.

   ▶ business letter requesting payment of an overdue bill _____

   ▶ blog post joking about the writer's high school reunion _____

   ▶ e-mail asking about the status of a purchase order _____

   ▶ student's journal entry about meeting her boyfriend's parents _____

   ▶ newspaper story about a City Council meeting _____

2. Write two or three well-developed **self-expressive** paragraphs in which you discuss one decision or action of which you're especially proud. The subject matter can be something that happened fairly recently or longer ago.

3. Write two or three well-developed **informative** paragraphs in which you explain how to perform a particular procedure with which you are familiar. The procedure might be something job-related, or something you were taught by a friend or family member, or even something you figured out on your own. Be sure to present the steps in the procedure in the order in which they must be performed.

4. Write two or three well-developed **interrogative** paragraphs in which you ask your academic advisor for information about a course you're required to take next semester. Request specific details. You might inquire about the teacher, the textbook, the scheduled days and times, the subject matter and workload, or anything else that might help you know what to expect.

5. Write two or three well-developed **persuasive** paragraphs in which you defend a particular belief of yours. As always when writing persuasively, you must present good arguments for your assertions, rather than simply venting.

6. Write a well-developed **entertaining** paragraph in which you attempt to amuse the reader. You might approach this through the self-expressive avenue, perhaps by relating an embarrassing or otherwise comical experience, or you may choose to tell a joke. In any case, however, avoid X-rated or otherwise objectionable subject matter.

CHAPTER 2

Audience

LEARNING OBJECTIVES

When you complete this chapter, you will be able to

- ► Identify your intended audience
- ► Analyze that audience to understand needs and expectations
- ► Accommodate the demands of the communication hierarchy: upward, lateral, and downward interaction

AUDIENCE IDENTIFICATION

After you have determined your purpose in writing, you must then ask yourself, "Who will read what I have written?" Just as a writer has one or more purposes for writing, every reader has one or more reasons for reading. This is important for a writer to bear in mind, because different audiences have different needs and expectations. For illustration, consider these two examples. The first is a text message from a college student to his friend, and the second is the body of an e-mail from that student to his professor.

Example #1

Dude—u wouldn't belive how sick i was after got home from that keg party thursday nite. puked my guts out, no way i could get 2 english class at 8 in the AM. no big deal we never do nothing anyways just a lot of crap about writting

Example #2

Dear Professor,

Please excuse my absence from your 8:00 a.m. English class on Friday. I was not feeling well and was therefore unable to attend. With your permission, I will of course make up any missed work.

Respectfully,

Eric Cartman

Obviously, these are two very different messages indeed! The first is highly informal and quite poorly written. Like so many hastily composed text messages, it's been thrown together in a totally careless manner, is flawed by typos and mechanical errors, and is guilty of the TMI ("too much information") blunder. Moreover, it's crudely worded and disturbingly unconcerned about the serious problems of alcohol abuse, irregular attendance, and academic indifference. Clearly, Eric does not expect these shortcomings to bother his friend. In fact, he may even be deliberately exaggerating in a misguided attempt to impress his friend with how "cool" he is. The e-mail, on the other hand, has been composed with much greater care and attention, reflecting Eric's desire to create an entirely different impression. Here he has taken pains to consider his audience and adjust his tone, correctly assuming that his professor will be a far more judgmental reader. It should be noted, however, that in general we do ourselves a disservice when we write sloppily, regardless of who's on the receiving end. Such writing creates a negative impression. We all make mistakes occasionally, but it's worth the added effort to eliminate *avoidable* errors caused by simple carelessness.

AUDIENCE ANALYSIS

Matters of correctness aside, it's important to consider the audience when determining what should be included—or left out—in a piece of writing. These questions will help you decide:

- ► Is my audience one person or more than one?
- ► What does my audience already know about this topic?
- ► How much do they care about it?
- ► Why do they need this information?
- ► What do I want them to understand, believe, feel, or do after reading?
- ► What factors might influence their response? For example, how about their age, gender, sexual orientation, racial/ethnic background, education level, interests, and beliefs?

Because these questions are closely related, the answers will necessarily overlap. But by examining your readers this way, you come to see the subject of your writing from their viewpoint as well as your own. As a result, you're better able to provide necessary details while eliminating unnecessary ones, cite meaningful examples, and achieve the correct level of formality. This enables you to avoid giving offense, prevent misunderstandings, and achieve the desired outcome.

But audience analysis can be tricky. While it's true that age, gender, and other such considerations do play a part in determining a reader's responses, every reader is still a unique individual. It would be mistaken to imagine that persons who share a given set of demographic characteristics all think alike. Nevertheless, certain broad assumptions can be made. For example, if you were writing a highly detailed description of some aspect of computer programming, the readers' education and interests would be important considerations, while their age and gender would be irrelevant. Your readers would have no difficulty with technical terminology and concepts if those readers were trained specialists in that field. But if they were not, then the description would have to include more background and be phrased far more simply, using everyday vocabulary.

COMMUNICATION HIERARCHY

Another feature of audience analysis is the need to consider the nature of your relationship to the reader. Although most of us would prefer a more democratic arrangement, not all human interaction occurs between equals. While much writing *is* intended for readers at your own level of responsibility or authority within the hierarchy, sometimes your reader is at a higher or lower level. Clearly, these differences strongly influence the tone of any piece of writing, as discussed in greater depth in Chapter 3. But for now, it's enough to acknowledge that all communication, written and otherwise, falls into several broad categories:

- ▶ **Upward communication:** Intended for those above the writer in the hierarchy, upward communication should adopt a very courteous approach that reflects the reader's authority over the writer. (Example: the student-to-professor e-mail shown earlier.)
- ▶ **Lateral communication:** Intended for those at the writer's own level in the hierarchy, lateral communication can adopt a much more casual, conversational approach that reflects the relative equality of reader and writer. (Example: the student-to-student text shown earlier.)
- ▶ **Downward communication:** Intended for those below the writer in the hierarchy, downward communication commonly adopts a firmer, more instructive approach that reflects the writer's authority over the reader. (Example: a performance evaluation written by a supervisor to an employee.)

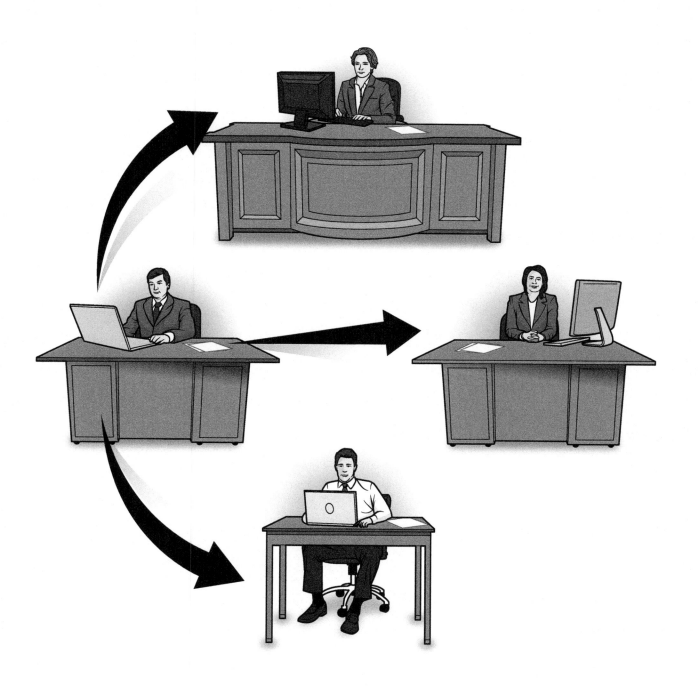

EXERCISES

1. Every newspaper, magazine, or other publication is aimed at a specific audience. Briefly identify the intended readers of the following periodicals. (If you're not familiar with these, you'll have to do some browsing in a library, at a magazine rack, or on the web.)

   Family Circle   The Onion
   Maxim   PMLA
   The New England Journal of Medicine   Runners World
   The New York Review of Books   USA Today
   The New Yorker   Weekly World News

2. The following is an online restaurant review. Identify the writer's intended audience.

   Imagine my surprise when I was told at the door of this Barcelona restaurant that my footwear was unacceptable! I had arrived wearing a pair of black leather Teva sandals popular among tourists. The receptionist looked at my feet and declared that I could not enter. My husband and I stood there while a manager was called. He reluctantly agreed that we could be seated. As unwelcome as we had been made to feel, and as puzzled as we were when we noticed that many of the younger guests were also wearing sandals and in some cases running shoes, it would have been difficult to enjoy even an excellent meal. But this one was far from that. The food was expensive but totally unremarkable, and the service was rushed and unprofessional from beginning to end. We thought that every other restaurant we visited during our month in Spain was much, much better.

3. Your audience is the president of your college. Write three paragraphs in which you attempt to convince the president to adopt, modify, or abandon a specific policy that impacts the daily lives of students.

4. Your audience is an eleventh- or twelfth-grade student at the high school from which you graduated. Write three paragraphs in which you explain the principal differences between high school and college.

5. Your audience is a classmate in English 101. Write three paragraphs in which you recommend a particular restaurant or nightclub.

CHAPTER 3

Tone

LEARNING OBJECTIVES

When you complete this chapter, you will be able to

▶ Employ a tone appropriate to your audience
▶ Convey an upbeat, reader-centered perspective
▶ Understand the difference between denotation and connotation
▶ Avoid gender-biased and other offensive language

TONE AND AUDIENCE

In academic writing, your audience is of course your professor (and perhaps your classmates, if group discussion of student work is part of the course format). But at the first-year level most professors of English usually expect students to compose as if they were writing for someone they didn't know—any reasonably intelligent and fairly well-informed stranger, though not necessarily a specialist in the topic area. Therefore, it's wise to pitch your writing that way unless your professor indicates otherwise. Maintain a fairly formal tone, avoiding overly conversational effects.

Elsewhere, however (on the job, let's say, or in your personal life), your actual relationship to your reader will determine your tone. But the tone of your writing—much like your tone of voice when you're speaking—is influenced by your purpose and also reflects your attitude toward the subject matter. This is especially true when writing about controversial issues, conveying "bad news" (the denial of a request from someone beneath you in the hierarchy, for example), or suggesting that someone should adopt some new or different procedure. Although writing in such situations can—indeed, *should*—be phrased in a firm, straightforward manner, a harsh, sarcastic, or belligerent approach is nearly always counterproductive. If your reader becomes defensive or resentful, communication breaks down. Therefore, don't try to sound tough or demanding when writing about sensitive issues. Instead, appeal to readers' best instincts, their sense of fairness and cooperation. Phrase sentences in a non-threatening way, acknowledging readers' potentially differing points of view while presenting enough concrete, factual detail to fully support your own position.

READER-CENTERED PERSPECTIVE

Also helpful is a reader-centered (rather than writer-centered) perspective. Here are examples of how to change a writer-centered perspective into a reader-centered one.

Writer-Centered	Reader-Centered
I am investigating the claim.	Your claim is being investigated.
We mailed the refund today.	Your refund was mailed today.
I assure you that…	You can be assured that…

Notice that using *you* and *your* rather than *I* and *we* personalizes the communication. Focusing on the reader this way is known as the "you" approach. Another important feature of reader-centeredness is the use of *please*, *thank you*, and other polite terms. Similarly, it's always best to strive for the most upbeat possible wording, especially when presenting unwelcome information. Here are examples of how to rephrase negative content in more positive, reader-centered terms.

Negative Wording	Positive Wording
We cannot complete your registration because the required deposit has not been received.	Your registration will be completed as soon as you submit the required deposit.
The restaurant is closed on Mondays.	The restaurant is open every day except Monday.
No children under the age of 12 are allowed in the hotel dining room.	Children age 12 and over are welcome in the hotel dining room.

What follows are two examples that illustrate these principles. Both e-mails have the same purpose—to change a specific behavior—and both address the same audience. But their tone differs greatly. The first adopts a writer-centered approach and is harshly combative. The reader-centered revision, on the other hand, is persuasively diplomatic and therefore much better. The first is almost certain to create resentment, whereas the second is far more likely to be well received.

Example #1

Date:	November 10, 2017
To:	All Students
From:	Dick Ketcham, Chief Campus Security
Subject:	Stolen Property

During the past couple of months my office has received a number of complaints about stolen purses, laptops, textbooks, and other items.

But it's become obvious that these events were the result of stupidity on the part of the so-called "victims." Trust me: If you leave stuff lying around in plain view and walk away for even a few minutes, it's going to grow legs. There are thieves all over the place on this campus.

And don't even get me started on burglaries of unlocked vehicles and dorm rooms. Come on, people—use your heads!

Example #2

Date: November 10, 2017

To: All Students

From: Dick Ketcham, Chief
            Campus Security

Subject: Protecting Your Property

Lately there have been increased reports of stolen purses, laptops, and other property.

For your own protection, never leave valuable personal belongings—including textbooks—unattended. In addition, always lock your vehicle and your dorm room. And if you see suspicious activity in the parking lots, dorms, or anywhere else on campus, please alert this office immediately.

With your help, my officers can continue to fulfill their mission—to serve and protect.

In most settings, you can adopt a somewhat more casual manner with your peers and with those below you than with those above you in the pecking order. Nevertheless, avoid an *excessively* conversational tone. Even if the situation isn't particularly troublesome or even when your reader is well-known to you, remember that writing is always somewhat more formal than speech, in part because it's more deliberate and far less impermanent. Although you need not sound stuffy, it's important to maintain a certain level of propriety. An especially polite tone is advisable when addressing those who outrank you, particularly when conveying unwelcome information or requesting assistance or cooperation from superiors. This can be achieved either through "softening" words and phrases (*perhaps, with your permission, if you wish*) or simply by stating outright that you fully understand that the decision is theirs. For example, consider these two e-mail messages.

Example #1

Date: November 11, 2017

To: Professor Sara Nac

From: Bud Weiser

Subject: Missed Class

Hey, Sara! You probably noticed that I blew off your class yesterday and wasn't there to hand in my essay assignment or take the quiz. No problem, I'll bring the paper to your office hours and take a make-up then. But don't bust my chops with penalties or any bull like that. Remember: My tuition pays your salary!

Example #2

Date: November 11, 2017

To: Professor Sara Nac

From: Bud Weiser

Subject: Missed Class

Hello, Professor. Please accept my apologies for missing class yesterday. I know there was an essay assignment due and also a quiz I missed. With your permission, I'll bring the paper to your office hours tomorrow. Would it be possible for me to make up the quiz then too? I realize there may be late penalties, but I'm hoping you might reconsider when I explain the reasons for my absence.

Although both deal with the same situation, the first is completely inappropriate in tone, so much so that it would likely result in negative consequences for the writer. With its far too-familiar salutation, its use of slang (*blew off…bust my chops…bull*), and its implication that the student, rather than the professor, can make the rules, it completely violates the norms of upward communication. By contrast, the second message is obviously much better because it's politely respectful, employs the "you" perspective, and properly reflects the nature of the relationship. In short, its courteous tone is far more likely to achieve the desired outcome.

DENOTATION AND CONNOTATION

In a related vein, all writers should understand the difference between denotation and connotation. The term *denotation* refers to the literal, dictionary definition of a word. *Connotation*, however, refers to the nuances and shades of meaning—the implications and associations—conveyed by a word. For example, *skinny* and *slim* mean essentially the same thing, but each of these terms has a different connotation, one negative and the other positive. To describe someone as skinny would be an insult, whereas describing someone as slim would be a compliment. It's important, therefore, to pay close attention to this aspect of wording. Connotation greatly affects the tone of a piece of writing and therefore influences the reader's responses. Consider, for example, the contrasting associations triggered by the following pairs of terms.

Positive or Neutral Connotation	Negative Connotation
athlete	jock
to object	to gripe
firm	stubborn
idealist	dreamer
inexpensive	cheap
reserved	aloof
thrifty	miserly
walk	swagger

BIASED LANGUAGE

Yet another important aspect of tone is the way in which writers handle gender issues. Since the 1960s we've come to understand that English (like most languages) tends to be male-oriented, as is the traditional view of society itself. However, men's and women's social roles have changed significantly. There are more women than men attending college today. Title IX legislation has promoted women's participation in sports. Women are working in many jobs from which they would've been excluded in the past. And in general we're evolving toward a more sophisticated, less restrictive sense of the relationship between the sexes—and of the issue of gender identity and sexual orientation as well.

Certainly we should try to use language in a way that mirrors these realities. After all, language not only reflects social values but also reinforces them. Clinging to old-fashioned constructions only perpetuates outdated attitudes.

Here are four examples of gender-biased writing:

▶   Every student must sign his name on the log-in sheet before beginning his tutoring.
▶   Mr. Lopez, Miss Carter, and Mrs. Madden will teach this course in the fall.
▶   The college Kiddie Kampus requests that each child's mother help out at lunch at least once a month.
▶   It will require six workmen to complete this painting job on time.

Although all of these sentences are grammatically correct, each is sexist. The first, by twice using the word *his*, implies that all students are male—certainly not the case in today's world! But the bias can be removed simply by cutting or changing a few words.

Every student must sign the log-in sheet before beginning tutoring.

In the second example, we can assume that Madden is married and Carter is single. But Lopez's marital status remains undetermined, as it should; such matters have no relevance to a person's professional role. Equal consideration should be granted to all three professors by referring to both women as Ms. or by dropping such titles altogether. In addition, names should always appear in alphabetical order unless there's a valid reason for some other sequence; in this case, there's no apparent reason why the male name should automatically stand first. Here are two possible revisions:

Ms. Carter, Mr. Lopez, and Ms. Madden will teach this course in the fall.
Professors Carter, Lopez, and Madden will teach this course in the fall.

The third sentence implies that childcare is solely the responsibility of mothers. A far better phrasing would be to replace *mother* with *parent(s)*:

The college Kiddie Kampus requests that each child's parent(s) help out at lunch at least once a month.

And, by using the word *workmen*, the last sentence implies that only males (work*men*) could do the job. Avoid gender-biased terms like *workman, fireman, mailman, policeman,* and the like. Instead, use gender-neutral ones like *worker, firefighter, mail carrier,* and *police officer.* Here's an example of that kind of revision:

It will require six painters to complete this job on time.

In the interest of simple fairness, we must all develop the habit of nonsexist expression. And, of course, it should go without saying that any kind of crude or vulgar language is entirely inappropriate in academic writing, as are the acronyms and similar shortcuts typical of text messages and tweets. This is not to suggest that academic writing should sound stiff or artificial, but that it should display intelligence, maturity, and sophistication. Accordingly, disrespectful terms that victimize individuals on the basis of race, religion, ethnicity, age, gender identity, sexual orientation, and physical and/or mental challenges are totally offensive and have absolutely no place in twenty-first century discourse. For in-depth advice on avoiding *unintentionally* disparaging language, consult Sections 3.12 to 3.17 of the *Publication Manual of the American Psychological Association,* available in any college library and on the web (www.apaa.org).

EXERCISES

1. Here are two e-mails. Each deals with the same issue. Which one is more likely to get the desired results? Why? Be specific.

Date: January 12, 2018

To: All Employees

From: James Almas
           Physical Plant Supervisor

Subject: Filthy Break Room

The Employee Break Room on the third floor of the Main Building is disgusting! The whole place is filthy. Nobody ever cleans up after cooking, so the microwave is caked with burned-on food, the refrigerator is always filled with rotting food, the sink is always stained and slimy, there's always garbage all over the floor, and the tables are always covered with crumbs and debris.

If things don't improve you'd better bet I'll tell management to close the Break Room indefinitely until people are ready to take responsibility for keeping it clean. My staff shouldn't have to kill themselves with unnecessary work!

Date: January 12, 2018

To: All Employees

From: James Almas
           Physical Plant Supervisor

Subject: Our Break Room

Certainly we all appreciate the amenities available in the Employee Break Room on the third floor of the Main Building. It's convenient to be able to store lunches in the refrigerator, use the microwave, and so forth. But I think you'll agree that the room is not always clean.

Of course, it's the responsibility of my staff to provide basic maintenance, but you can help us greatly just by following a few simple procedures:

► Leave food in the refrigerator for no more than a few days
► Clean up any spills inside the microwave
► Rinse out the sink after using it
► Put all garbage into the waste receptacle
► Use dampened paper towels to wipe off the tables

Thanks for your cooperation, which will ensure a more pleasant atmosphere for us all!

2. In general, a positive tone is preferable to a negative one. Using the following example as a model, revise each of these sentences to create a more upbeat tone.

<u>We close</u> at 5:30.   REVISION: <u>We stay open</u> until 5:30.
negative   positive

▶ Your diploma cannot be mailed until you pay the graduation fees.

_____

▶ This office is not open on Fridays.

_____

▶ We have run out of the eggplant special. All we have off the menu is the fish fry.

_____

▶ If the fire alarm bells ring, do not panic.

_____

▶ No new purchases can be authorized until the budget is approved.

_____

▶ Please don't forget to turn off your computer when you leave work.

_____

▶ We have received your paperwork but are unable to respond until July 1.

_____

▶ If you have any questions, don't hesitate to e-mail me.

_____

3. Revise the following sentences to eliminate gender-biased language. (One is already correct.)

▶ Any man who wants to be well-informed about current events should read *The New York Times* every day.

_____

▶ A student enrolled in college should understand the importance of completing all his assignments on time.

_____

▶ An employee's job satisfaction is usually related to his interest in the work.

_____

▶ Every American president has tried to surround himself with highly competent advisors.

_____

▶ When a mailman approaches a residence, he should watch out for loose dogs.

_____

▶ I now pronounce you man and wife.

_____

▶ A motorcyclist must never ride with his kickstand extended.

_____

▶ In general, man-made materials are less expensive than natural ones.

_____

▶ Men who pursue law or medicine usually earn a substantial income.

_____

▶ A policeman should use his pistol only if he has no alternative.

_____

PART 2

The Writing Process: Pre-Writing, Drafting, Rewriting

More than thirty years ago, James C. Raymond, then a professor at the University of Alabama, published a book called *Writing Is an Unnatural Act*. Professor Raymond wasn't just joking around, trying to boost sales on the strength of a catchy title. He was onto something very fundamental: Writing is difficult and must be learned, mainly because it is indeed unnatural. If it were not, we'd each be born with ink in our index finger.

Granted, speech too is a learned activity. But the impulse to speak is instinctive. Writing, on the other hand, is quite different. It might almost be described as an artificial *substitute* for speech. As such, it's not instinctive. Rather, it's a highly conscious activity involving deliberate choices determined by principles and rules that must be gradually absorbed and then carefully applied. And, like anything requiring a learned skill (playing a sport or a musical instrument, for example) it must be practiced. Nobody can produce good writing without understanding this and putting in the necessary effort.

Because of reluctance to confront this very basic aspect of composition, many students attempt to write as if they were simply speaking aloud. As a result, their essays are unfocused, disorganized, and poorly developed. Not surprisingly, their grades are disappointing. Other students, though, get better results, earning a good grade on every assignment. Their secret? Somewhere along the way they've learned to accept the fact that writing is not natural and automatic. They know that it's instead a process, a three-step operation involving not only drafting (which is actually just the middle step) but also pre-writing and rewriting. To ignore this is like trying to make a sandwich without the bread. This section of the book explores each of the three steps and provides detailed recommendations.

CHAPTER 4

Pre-Writing

LEARNING OBJECTIVES

When you complete this chapter, you will be able to

- ► Use pre-writing strategies such as brainstorming, freewriting, topic mapping, and exploring outside sources
- ► Create an effective thesis statement
- ► Focus, organize, and outline your subject matter

PRE-WRITING STRATEGIES

Like a competitive runner performing a stretching routine before racing, a writer should warm up before attempting to compose. Just as the athlete employs a variety of exercises, the writer should also complete some preliminary activities. Foremost among these is simply thinking about the subject. Whether your professor has assigned a particular topic or allowed you to choose your own, you'll need to develop your ideas and begin to organize your approach. Time permitting, it's very helpful to consider the general subject for a day or two before actually picking up your pen or sitting down at the computer. Try to give the topic some thought while engaged in unrelated activities requiring little or no attention (taking a shower, folding the laundry, waiting for a bus). Then, when you do eventually attempt to write, you'll have something to bring to the table. This is much better than the discouraging predicament of facing the blank page or screen with an equally empty head. But there won't be much time for this preliminary thinking if you ignore the assignment until the night before it's due. Always get started as soon as possible.

Unfortunately, thinking is not always enough. Ideas may not occur to you as quickly as you'd like or you may have trouble coming up with any ideas at all. But *brainstorming, freewriting, idea mapping,* and *exploring outside sources* can be effective strategies to get your mental wheels turning and start the writing process.

Brainstorming

This involves putting pen to paper—or fingers to keyboard—without a plan and with as little conscious thought as possible. In the workplace, this is often done collaboratively by teams of employees as a way to solve problems or develop new approaches to familiar tasks. In academic settings it can be similarly used by students working on group projects. But in either environment it's equally helpful to the individual writer, as a way of breaking through whatever obstacles may be interfering with getting started.

If you have no topic yet, you can begin with a random list of things you *might* want to write about. Don't analyze or judge ("this would be good…that's a dumb idea") at this point. Just quickly list, without evaluating, whatever comes to mind. You may discover one or two possible topics to explore further in another brainstorm or another pre-writing activity. If you do have a topic, or if you've just come up with a possibility, write it at the top of a blank sheet of paper or type it at the top of your screen. Then, in list format, write down whatever related words or phrases come to mind. Again, don't question or eliminate. Just jot everything down. In a few minutes, after you've run out of steam, look back over what you've got. Most likely you'll start to see things you can work with.

The brainstorm below is the result of a student's decision to explore her first job as a possible essay topic.

My first job

huge brick factory building	lots of laughs
noisy assembly line	line goes too fast
roaches in lockers	good pay in cash envelope
shoes not sandals	basketball courts next door
no air conditioning	luncheonette
summer heat	assembling parts
power tools	blind co-worker
loud machines	cafeteria for coffee, toast
dirty	two blocks to subway
can't figure out job	union walkout
cool co-workers, helpful	cross picket line?

You'll notice that some thoughts seem related and others do not. The list is basically a catalog of random details that came to mind when she began thinking about the experience. But it proved helpful because as she considered the list she discovered her focus. She realized that what she really wanted to write about was how that first job experience helped shape her attitudes toward labor unions. This might then lead to another pre-writing activity—*freewriting*.

Freewriting

Another way to generate material, this is not unlike brainstorming, in that you allow whatever comes to mind to appear on your paper or screen. But in freewriting you take a more headlong approach, writing sentences and phrases non-stop for a set period of time.

To freewrite, give yourself five minutes, set a timer, and write continuously until the five minutes are up. Don't erase, don't cross out, don't pause or stop to think. Don't worry about typos, grammar, spelling, or punctuation. (Remember: This writing is *free*.) Just keep moving. If your mind goes blank, write "I can't think of anything" or "I don't know what to write." You may surprise yourself when you see ideas emerge that you hadn't realized were there.

Freewriting can be done alone, as the only pre-writing for a given essay. Alternatively, it can be done in conjunction with other activities, to expand or find yet another path to the essay you want to write. The freewriting that follows was an outgrowth of the brainstorm above. Doing this other, different kind of pre-writing allowed the student to again explore the "first job" topic, but this time with an eye toward how it influenced her thoughts about unions.

That was really something, that walkout. I had no idea it was coming. Up from the subway one morning and there they were. All my co-workers in the street. Handmade signs, talking together, smoking, walking up and down. Like a picket line. Should I go in? Not a union member, just a summer employee. But these were the people who helped me out every day. I was clueless about how to do the work. They helped me on the assembly line, did their work faster and then helped me with mine. Cheered me up. Warned me about the roaches. This day, they said, "Go on in! It's okay, you need the money for college." But I couldn't. Even though I knew my family wouldn't be happy about it—wouldn't look good, give up that day's pay. But something made me stay out. Stayed on the sidewalk. Hoped it would help. Solidarity? Maybe topic.

Although a jumble of thoughts and ideas, this second pre-writing still brought the student closer to the focus, organization, and development that would eventually emerge from the writing process.

Topic Mapping

This pre-writing strategy presents ideas within circles or ovals linked by lines or arrows, placing related thoughts near each other, showing the relationships among ideas. It's especially useful for visual learners, but can help any writer begin to organize thoughts.

One way to make a topic map is to write a topic in a circle or oval in the center of the page and begin to surround it with several others enclosing ideas you may want to discuss. Each of these can in turn be surrounded by yet another cluster identifying sub-points within the original ideas. Lines or arrows can reinforce the relationships among main ideas and supporting ideas. This approach not only helps you to generate ideas, but also begins to organize them, the next step in creating a rough draft.

Some writers prefer to enclose their ideas within squares, rectangles, or triangles rather than circles or ovals, but the example that follows is a more typical, oval-based topic map.

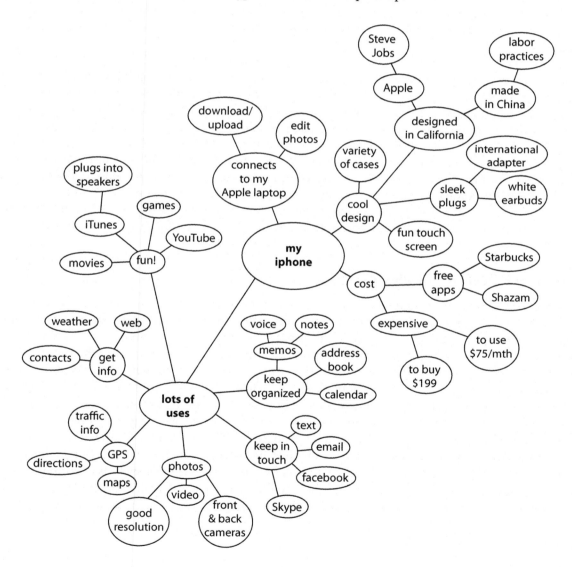

In this example, the student began with "my iPhone" as a possible topic for writing. Then he used ovals and connecting lines to lay out whatever ideas came to him. He didn't try to analyze them too deeply as he went, and he didn't worry about whether everything would be useful in the end. He simply put things down on the paper.

Through this mapping he discovered many related ideas that could lead to a variety of possible essays. Could he use all of these ideas in one 500–750 word paper? Obviously not. But from them he might begin to develop a descriptive essay about the iPhone's appearance, a process analysis about how to use iPhone features to stay in touch with friends, a research paper about the labor practices of Apple suppliers in China, or an exemplification essay about the reasons why company founder Steve Jobs was so important to the success of Apple products. The possibilities are many, and laying thoughts out in a non-linear way like this can make it easier for a writer to see them.

Exploring Outside Sources

This approach can also get your thoughts flowing, but it should not be confused with the type of formal research and documentation required when writing an in-depth, research-based term paper. Rather, it's an informal, "getting acquainted" process that can be useful when you have to write an assigned essay on an unfamiliar subject.

For example, let's say your professor has assigned the topic, "Dress Codes in the Workplace." It's not intended to be a research paper, but simply one in which you express your own point of view. But you may not have given this subject much thought before. You may not have firm opinions about it, even if you've worked jobs requiring the observance of such rules. In a case like this, it makes sense to consult outside sources. These may include people knowledgeable about the topic, newspaper or magazine articles, TV, radio, and other media, or—and this is of course the quickest and easiest source available—the Web. A Google search for this subject yields nearly three million hits. Not all are reliable, and no one could consult them all even if they were. But just by reading the headings of the links you can start to develop a better sense of the subject's range and complexity. For example, you might find information about restrictions on body modifications such as piercings and tattoos, and employers' responses to various circumstances requiring rule modifications or exceptions. Such angles may not have occurred to you before, but are now available for your use.

CREATING AN EFFECTIVE THESIS STATEMENT

Whatever pre-writing strategies you use, you'll eventually discover what you want to say by considering all the ideas that have surfaced. At that point you must formulate your *thesis statement*, one sentence that clearly identifies not only your topic but what you'll say about it. This is the "controlling idea" of the essay. Highly skilled writers sometimes employ an *implied* thesis, presenting it indirectly, especially when the topic is some sort of no-brainer. The writer of a paper about the absurdity of Holocaust denial, for example, can safely assume that readers will get the point without having it spelled out in the introduction. Indeed, in a case like that, the very title of the piece has probably established the thesis already. Far more typically, however, there is a firmly phrased thesis statement, especially in a paper written to satisfy a college assignment.

Although it can appear elsewhere—sometimes even as the very first sentence—the thesis is usually positioned at the end of the introduction, after the reader has discovered your general topic. But it's the thesis itself that informs the reader about your focus and your point of view. Since your purpose is to communicate all of this to your readers, keeping their interest and earning their trust are essential. Different types of essays call for certain specific elements in a thesis, as you'll see in later chapters, but broad rules do apply.

Phrase your thesis as an assertion

It can be said that every piece of writing is an exercise in persuasion, in the sense that all writing tries to convince the reader to keep reading. Therefore, a good thesis statement is phrased as a reasonable assertion, a sentence that expresses a complete thought about the subject of your essay. It does not simply announce the topic ("This essay will attempt to prove that X is preferable to Y."). Instead, it makes a claim such as "X is preferable to Y because Z." Here are some examples of this approach:

▶ The electoral college should be abolished because it unnecessarily complicates the voting process.
▶ The drinking age should be lowered to eighteen nationwide because eighteen-year-olds are permitted to drive, marry, and serve in the military.
▶ Every college campus should be totally tobacco-free because this would result in health benefits for smokers and non-smokers alike.

Phrase your thesis in a reasonable, even-handed way

Although your thesis statement should be a firm expression of your intentions, *over*statement will alienate your readers rather than engage them. For example, consider these two thesis statements. Both are on the same topic and both are in fundamental agreement, but the second is much too aggressive

▶ Although some people are opposed to helmet laws for motorcyclists, all the evidence shows that helmets save riders' lives.

  NOT

▶ Anybody who's opposed to helmet laws for motorcyclists is a complete idiot.

Thanks to its more appropriate tone, the first of these thesis statements is far more likely to be taken seriously, even by readers who disagree.

Focus on only one thing

Since the thesis expresses a point of view, it must focus on only one aspect of the topic. For example, consider the topic of having a job while going to college. Are there both advantages and disadvantages to doing this? Surely so. But unless you're writing a comparison/contrast essay (see Chapter 8), you should focus on either one or the other, not both.

▶ Working while going to college is a bad idea for several reasons.

  OR

▶ Working while going to college helps students develop habits that will be useful to them for the rest of their lives.

  NOT

▶ There are advantages and disadvantages to working while going to college.

A narrower focus enables you to show your reader in greater depth and more specifically why it's good *or* why it's bad. You're not just providing information. As a writer, you have to decide what you want to communicate to your reader, what your focus is going to be, what your perspective is on this topic. Your thesis statement firms this up, and it's a key part of what makes your essay an essay.

Show how your essay will be developed

Essays can be developed in a variety of ways, as we shall see in later chapters. Part of the work of the thesis statement is to let your reader know from the beginning what type of development to expect. Will you tell a story? Define a term? Describe a place or person? Compare? Contrast? Explain a procedure? The thesis should make clear what approach your essay will take, whatever it is. "Renting a house at the Jersey Shore can be easy and affordable if you follow these steps" prepares the reader for an essay that explains a procedure, but "Renting a house at the Jersey Shore turned into a nightmare for my family" signals a very different kind of essay—one that tells a story.

Be prepared to revise your thesis as necessary

Your thesis is not necessarily permanent. It can be a work in progress. The essay may take you in unexpected directions as it unfolds. If that happens, don't resist. As the twentieth century British novelist E.M. Forster once asked, "How do I know what I think till I see what I say?" Let the discussion develop as it must. When you reach the rewriting stage, it's much easier to revise the thesis to match the essay than it would be to revise the essay to match the thesis.

FOCUSING, ORGANIZING, OUTLINING

Once you've completed your pre-writing and settled on a thesis, you must now begin the related tasks of focusing and organizing. Try to determine which ideas are closely related. Almost always, several will be. Combine them. This will make your job more manageable, by giving you fewer ideas to deal with. Next, rank-order your ideas: most important first, least important last. Then eliminate the last idea or two in the bottom of the rankings. Anything that unimportant to you is probably not worth mentioning. Besides, there won't be room for it. Now you'll have what you really need: several main ideas that will provide adequate content with which to support your thesis.

For the sake of illustration, let's say you're writing about the topic "What I'd Do If I Won a Million Dollars." Here's how your subject matter might evolve:

Stage 1	Stage 2	Stage 3	Stage 4
buy new car	car, house	debts, investments	debts, investments
buy new house	New York	New York	New York
visit New York City	debts, stocks	car, house	car, house
pay off school loans	family, church	family, church	family, church
pay off credit cards	Europe	Europe	
invest in stock market			
give $ to parents			
give $ to sister			
give $ to church			
travel to Europe			

Just as you used pre-writing strategies to determine which sub-points to cover in your essay about the larger topic, you must now go one step farther. Using those same strategies, assemble details about each sub-point so that the body paragraphs of your essay will be sufficiently developed. To illustrate once again, your "Million Dollars" subject might generate details like these:

Topics	Supporting Details
Debts	student loans (state college, community college): $10,000
	Master Card (unnecessary purchases): $5,000
	Visa (Spring Break): $3,000
Investments	stocks (G.E., Apple, Google): $50,000
New York City	shopping (clothes, jewelry, accessories), sightseeing (Empire State Bldg, Statue of Liberty, Ground Zero, Central Park, Metropolitan Museum, etc.): $35,000
Car	red Miata (six-speed, Pirellis): $35,000
House	mountain location, 10–12 acres, central air, game room, pool: $700,000
Family	parents (Florida vacation, retirement fund): $100,000
	sister (cash gift): $50,000
Church	social room renovations, parking lot blacktop: $10,000

You must now decide how to organize your essay. If your topic is chronological in nature (for example, "What I Did on New Year's Eve") this is fairly easy. You simply tell the story, after first deciding how to compress the events by determining which details to *leave out*—always a key decision when writing. But if your topic is not chronological (for example, "Three Reasons Why Extreme Fighting Should Be Outlawed"), you must identify the most effective sequence for your ideas. In general, the way to structure such an essay is to use *ascending order of importance*, following a "good/better/best" approach, saving your most convincing material for last. This pattern enables the paper to gain momentum as it moves along, building the interest level ever higher at each point along the way.

Non-chronological essays are typically structured in this ascending order because human psychology prefers that kind of progression. Almost everything in life operates accordingly. A fancy dinner starts with the appetizer, not the main dish. A rock concert opens with a lesser-known band before the headliners take the stage. And you can probably come up with many other examples on your own. A useful strategy for finding the best sequencing of ideas is to create an index card or sticky note for each. These can be physically arranged and rearranged until the ideal pattern emerges. Of course, many writers prefer to do this electronically, "cutting and pasting" on the computer to try out various possibilities.

Some students prefer (and many professors require) a working outline, an orderly system of headings and sub-headings that enable material to be organized in a highly visual way. Major headings are flush with the left margin and identified with Roman numerals, while sub-headings are identified with capital letters, Arabic numerals, and lowercase letters, in that order. Indenting is used to further reinforce the relationships among the headings. Here's how a working outline of the "Million Dollars" paper might look (see following page).

I – Introduction
II – Finances
  A. Debts
    1. Student loans
    2. Master Card
    3. Visa
  B. Stocks
    1. General Electric
    2. Google
    3. Apple
III – New York City Trip
  A. Shopping
    1. Clothes
    2. Jewelry
    3. Accessories
  B. Sightseeing
    1. Empire State Building
    2. Statue of Liberty
    3. Ground Zero
    4. Central Park
    5. Metropolitan Museum
IV – Car, House
  A. Car
    1. Mazda Miata
      a. Six-speed transmission
      b. Pirelli tires
  B. House
    1. Mountain location
    2. Two acres
    3. Central air-conditioning
    4. Fully-equipped game room
      a. pool table
      b. sound system
      c. electronic games
    5. Swimming pool
V – Parents, Sister, Church
  A. Parents
    1. Florida vacation
    2. Retirement fund
  B. Sister
    1. Shopping trip
    2. Cash gift
  C. Church
    1. Social room renovation
    2. Parking lot re-surfacing
VI – Conclusion

It's not always so easy to decide whether a given topic should be approached chronologically or not. Our "Million Dollars" essay is a case in point. It might depend on what the writer would actually do "in real life." But ascending order of importance would be helpful in making this somewhat routine topic as interesting as possible. Should the writer really follow the sequence shown in the above outline or would some other order be better? This may depend on what the thesis finally turns out to be. Indeed, the kind of deliberation that would be necessary for the writer to decide is an example of how writing is in many ways an exercise in decision-making. And it also illustrates the truth of E.M. Forster's comment that we don't really know what we think about something until we try to write about it. The very act of composition serves to clarify our thinking. It's not unusual for a writer to revise not only a thesis, but also a working outline to reflect changes as the essay evolves.

Of course, one writer's treatment of a given subject will differ greatly from another's. Every writer operates from a unique perspective. But regardless of the subject or your approach to it, the pre-writing activities discussed here will help. Time-consuming as they may seem, they will make the drafting stage of the process much easier and will actually *save* you time then.

EXERCISES

1. Here are five essay topics that a professor might assign:

   ▶ A Very Angry Moment
   ▶ Employment Opportunities in My Field of Study
   ▶ A Brief History of [choose your favorite sport or hobby]
   ▶ Capital Punishment: Right or Wrong?
   ▶ The Person Who Has Most Influenced My Life

   Which of these topics are chronological in nature? Create a working outline for one of them.

2. Choose any one of the topics in Exercise 1 and create a topic map for it.

3. Choose any one of the topics in Exercise 1 and create a thesis statement for it.

   _____

   _____

4. Here are five thesis statements. Not all are satisfactory. Identify the unsatisfactory ones and rewrite them.

   ▶ Last summer my family spent our vacation at Disney World.

   _____

   ▶ Many people's objections to President Obama's policies were motivated by racism, their discomfort at seeing an African-American in the White House.

   _____

   _____

   ▶ Working as a "front of the house" receptionist in a restaurant is similar in some ways to being a member of the wait staff, but in many other ways it's very different.

   _____

   _____

   ▶ The famous short story "The Necklace" is about a woman who loses some borrowed jewelry.

   _____

   _____

► Abortion is nothing more than legalized murder.

_____

_____

5. Here is an introductory paragraph from a student essay. Although well-written, it's incomplete because it has no thesis statement. Provide one.

A recent study published in the journal *Pediatrics* has shown that excessive exposure to television is even more harmful to young children than previously acknowledged. According to this study, the average child eight months to eight years old spends eighty minutes per day actively watching t.v., and is exposed to nearly four additional hours of background television noise. The study claims that this causes decreased attention spans, lower cognitive skills, and reduced parent-child interaction.

_____

_____

_____

CHAPTER 5

Drafting

LEARNING OBJECTIVES

When you complete this chapter, you will be able to

- ► Create a concise but meaningful essay title
- ► Craft an effective introduction that gets the reader's attention, identifies the topic, and states the thesis
- ► Write unified, coherent, well-developed body paragraphs that successfully demonstrate the validity of the thesis
- ► Write an effective conclusion that gracefully closes the discussion

CREATING A MEANINGFUL TITLE

Imagine how difficult it would be to find your favorite breakfast cereal in the supermarket if there were no product names on the boxes—just shelf after shelf of identical packages, with no way to tell hot cereal from cold, sweetened from unsweetened, or even Wheaties from Cheerios. How about your local multiplex movie theater? What if there were no film titles above the various doors? How would you know which viewing room to enter after buying your ticket? For that matter, how could you decide which stories to read in your home-town newspaper—whether hard copy or electronic—if there were no headlines? Clearly, all these situations would be quite unsatisfactory, and all for the same reason. The cereal boxes, the rooms, and the stories all need "labels" to indicate what's inside. The same is true of an essay. It must have a title that signals what it's about, thereby orienting the reader by providing a sense of what to expect.

Unfortunately, however, not all titles are created equal. Many are unhelpful because they're vague or incomplete. A title such as "Capital Punishment," for example, provides no clue as to where the discussion may be heading. Is the writer for or against the death sentence, or somewhere in-between? Certainly, "Capital Punishment: Legalized Murder" (or, conversely, "Capital Punishment: An Eye for an Eye") would be much better. Note that both of these revisions achieve their purpose by using a colon to create a two-part title in which the second half expands upon the first. This is a very useful strategy.

Let's consider once again the "Million Dollars" essay discussed in Chapter 4. The student knew that the paper would explore possible uses of a large monetary windfall. But the first several titles that suggested themselves during the pre-writing stage of composition were unsatisfactory. The first was "A Cool Million." Next was "A Dollar and a Dream." The student realized that although both of these working titles were catchy, neither really conveyed fully what the essay was about. The first could be misinterpreted in a number of ways, perhaps even as relating to American author Nathanael West's highly-regarded 1934 novel of that name. The second could suggest that the essay was about the New York State Lottery, which uses that phrase as a slogan. So the student decided to play it straight, settling on "A Million Dollars." But that revision also left something to be desired, again because it could be interpreted in a great many ways. Eventually she decided to simply compress the content of her introduction, settling on, "What I'd Do With A Million Dollars: Wise Choices." This final revision is far better than the earlier versions, because it's clear and straightforward, allowing no opportunity for misinterpretation.

The same principle applies when you're writing about literature. A title such as "Romeo and Juliet" serves no purpose except to reveal which work you're discussing. It gives no indication of what the essay might have to say about Shakespeare's great tragedy. Indeed, a vague title like that is almost always an indication that the writer doesn't really know where the essay is headed. It usually accompanies a paper that lacks a real thesis statement and is nothing more than plot summary, a re-telling of the story, with little or no analysis or interpretation. This guarantees a low grade. So that's another feature of the title: to orient not only the reader but the writer as well. If you're having trouble coming up with a good title, you probably don't really know what you're trying to accomplish in the paper and should return to the pre-writing stage.

CRAFTING AN EFFECTIVE INTRODUCTION

The first thing to understand about the introduction to an essay is that it's simply a beginning and nothing more. You should not start the actual discussion of your topic until the *second* paragraph. The introductory paragraph is like first gear. You use it to pull away from the curb, not to drive down the street. Its purpose is only to get the reader's attention, identify the topic, and state the thesis. Granted, your title should already have suggested some of the essay's concerns, but the introduction—usually with its thesis statement at or near the end—firmly establishes the essay's direction.

A typical paragraph is approximately five or six sentences long, not just one, and the introduction is no exception. As stated above, it should identify the topic and state the thesis, but it must first get the reader's attention. This is important, because the opening sentence or two create the influential "first impression" the reader receives. Typically, the introduction opens broadly and becomes increasingly specific, funneling down until the writer reaches the thesis statement. Most good introductions follow that "general to specific" pattern. How, then, might the writer come up with four or five sentences that will lead effectively into the thesis statement? Here are three proven strategies that can help you get that job done.

Opening Attention Getter

THESIS

Describe a situation

There's something in human nature that loves a story, especially if it involves conflict. The enduring appeal of fairy tales, myths and legends, soap operas, and sentimental country-western song lyrics proves the point. Even jokes—which nearly always involve conflict—are a kind of story! You can capitalize on this aspect of your reader's psychology by opening with a brief anecdote that somehow relates to your subject. An essay exploring the dangers of tobacco, for example, might begin like this:

> My friend Carol was a smart, beautiful young woman with a bright future, but she had one bad habit. She'd been smoking a pack of cigarettes every day since ninth grade. When I attended our class reunion ten years after graduation, I was looking forward to seeing her again, but she wasn't there. Then I learned the sad truth. Carol had died of lung cancer shortly after her twenty-fifth birthday! But this didn't have to happen. If she'd kicked the habit she'd probably still be alive today.

Present an interesting fact or statistic

This will help you get the reader's attention by demonstrating that you're familiar with your topic. The annual edition of the *World Almanac and Book of Facts* is a rich source of statistical information on diverse topics, but there are many others as well. Any qualified librarian can direct you to government documents, corporate reports, and other useful resources. Even though statistics can be deceptive, people like what they perceive as the hard reality of such data and therefore find numbers quite persuasive. Although many Internet sites are untrustworthy, the web is another good source of statistics if used selectively. One useful website is *Statistical Resources on the Web* at www.lib.umich.edu/govdocs/stats.html. Another is the U.S. Department of Labor's Bureau of Labor Statistics at www.bls.gov/home.html. But there's one important point to remember if you want to retain credibility when citing a statistic. You must somehow acknowledge the source, usually on a Works Cited page at the end. Alternatively, you can identify a source in the body of the paper. Here's how an essay intended to demonstrate the need for stricter gun control legislation might open using this strategy:

> According to the Congressional Record, there are more than 35,000 handgun-related murders in the United States every year. In Japan, on the other hand, there are fewer than twenty. Of course, there are many reasons for this striking contrast. For one thing, Japan is an ancient, essentially monolithic culture in which most people share the same fundamental assumptions and beliefs, a fact that tends to discourage overt interpersonal conflict. As a result, violent crime in general is far less common in Japan. But the biggest reason for the difference is that in Japan the private ownership of firearms is strictly regulated. Clearly, it's time for the United States to re-think our self-destructive love affair with guns.

Use a quotation

Get a "Big Name"—Shakespeare, Martin Luther King, Jr., the Bible—to speak for you. Find an appropriate saying that will launch your own remarks with flair. Many useful books of quotations exist, but *Bartlett's Familiar Quotations* is surely the best known, and for good reason. Bartlett's includes nearly one hundred quotes on the subject of money alone, for example. It's available in any library or good bookstore and on the web, along with *Simpson's Contemporary Quotations* and the *Columbia World of Quotations*. As with statistics, you should always identify the source. And try to choose sources that your intended reader will be familiar with and fairly trustful of. Opening an academic essay with lyrics from an obscure Megadeath song, for example, probably won't win you any extra credit. Here's the kind of introduction that might, if you were writing an essay about climate change:

> As former vice-president Al Gore tells us in his best-selling 2006 book *An Inconvenient Truth,* "Not only does human-caused global warming exist, but it is also growing more and more dangerous, and at a pace that has now made it a planetary emergency." Yet there remain a great many skeptics who reject Gore's claims and those of the world's scientists, nearly all of whom agree that global warming constitutes a real, immediate, and potentially far-reaching threat. For whatever reason, these nay-sayers refuse to accept the obvious. Clearly, it's imperative that the United States take a leading role in the developed world's efforts to prevent environmental catastrophe.

As mentioned in Chapter 4 and illustrated above, the thesis statement most commonly appears at or near the end of the introduction. There are, however, exceptions to this loose rule. Some writers prefer to actually open with the thesis, or embed it somewhere within the introduction. This can sometimes be very effective. Notice, for example, that moving the thesis statement in the above introduction about global warming in no way damages the paragraph's integrity.

Opening Thesis

Clearly, it's imperative that the United States take a leading role in the developed world's efforts to prevent environmental catastrophe. As former vice-president Al Gore tells us in his best-selling 2006 book *An Inconvenient Truth*, "Not only does human-caused global warming exist, but it is also growing more and more dangerous, and at a pace that has now made it a planetary emergency." Yet there remain a great many skeptics who reject Gore's claims and those of the world's scientists, nearly all of whom agree that global warming constitutes a real, immediate, and potentially far-reaching threat. For whatever reason, these nay-sayers refuse to accept the obvious.

Embedded Thesis

As former vice-president Al Gore tells us in his best-selling 2006 book *An Inconvenient Truth*, "Not only does human-caused global warming exist, but it is also growing more and more dangerous, and at a pace that has now made it a planetary emergency." Clearly, it's imperative that the United States take a leading role in the developed world's efforts to prevent environmental catastrophe. Yet there remain a great many skeptics who reject Gore's claims and those of the world's scientists, nearly all of whom agree that global warming constitutes a real, immediate, and potentially far-reaching threat. For whatever reason, these nay-sayers refuse to accept the obvious.

When embedding the thesis, it's necessary to place it in the best possible location. Consider again the global warming example. If the thesis had been positioned as the third sentence in the paragraph, it would have been misplaced, disrupting the flow by creating an interruption between the two sentences about climate change deniers. So the placement of an embedded thesis requires careful deliberation. For this reason, most student writers find it easier to simply adopt the conventional practice of placing the thesis statement at the end of the introduction.

BODY PARAGRAPHS

Technically, an essay has no set length. The great nineteenth century American poet/philosopher Ralph Waldo Emerson wrote essays that are dozens of pages long. In general, though, a typical college-level essay is far shorter, usually only two or three double-spaced pages and rarely more than five. After the introduction, the writer provides several "body paragraphs" that demonstrate the validity of the thesis statement provided at the outset. An essay—like nearly every other kind of writing—is broken down into paragraphs, rather than simply pushing ahead in one long, relentless surge of text. This is because readers comprehend better when information is segmented into separate sections. We read in much the same way we normally eat: one bite at a time, chewing and swallowing before moving on to the next mouthful.

Indeed, the word "paragraph" has an interesting history that reinforces this basic concept. Hundreds of years ago, before the printing press had been invented or paragraphing as we know it had been developed, the medieval monks were responsible for creating handwritten manuscripts of sacred texts. They understood that readers prefer to digest information a little at a time. So they'd place a small drawing (a flower or a crucifix, for example) in the margin of the page as a signal to the reader when a new idea was beginning. These illustrations were called paragraphs, from the Latin *para* ("alongside of") and the Greek *gra'fo* ("writing"). Eventually these time-consuming drawings were replaced by the more efficient practice of simply beginning each new idea with indentation—some empty space. Thus was born what we now (somewhat inaccurately) call the paragraph.

Topic Sentences and Support Sentences

A good body paragraph should include a topic sentence identifying the paragraph's main idea, reinforced by a series of support sentences. Although the topic sentence sometimes appears elsewhere, it's usually the first sentence in the paragraph. For example, consider how the first (topic) sentence in the above paragraph sets the stage for what follows, a brief history. Notice also that the above paragraph is seven sentences long. That's fairly typical, although a paragraph can run a bit longer, especially if some of the sentences are very short. A good rule of thumb is that a paragraph in an essay should be roughly 100–150 words long.

Unity and Coherence

Because a good paragraph achieves unity by dealing only with the one main idea identified in its topic sentence, all the support sentences must relate directly to that idea. In addition, each of those support sentences should be sufficiently well-developed. This is done by providing factual data of a concrete, specific nature. For example, it's better to say *four* rather than *a few*, or *red, yellow, and orange* rather than *colorful*. Just as crucially, the paragraph must be coherently organized, so the support sentences must appear in the most logical sequence. Here is a body paragraph from the final version of the million dollar essay. Notice how it reflects the principles explained above. It focuses on one thing and one only, identified in the topic sentence. The support sentences that follow contain much specific detail and they appear in a logical, orderly sequence.

> Next would be my charge cards. When I got my Master Card in high school I spent more than $500 on a fancy wristwatch for a boy I was dating. Then there were other unwise spending sprees, so now the card is at its limit of $5,000. My Visa Card is also a disaster. I ran that one up after I could no longer use the Master Card. Last year I went to Florida with my girlfriends on spring break. They had no money so I covered a lot of our expenses, incurring more debt of nearly $2,000.

Just as the sentences within a paragraph should appear in the best possible order, so should the body paragraphs themselves. And the relationships among the main ideas of each can be clarified by the use of transition words and phrases. Transitions can serve as links between sentences, but can also be used at the beginning of a paragraph (as in the above paragraph, which opens with the transition "Next") to create a bridge between what's just been said and what lies ahead. This is highly important to consider when you reach the rewriting stage of composition.

What's been said so far applies to the body paragraphs of an essay, but these principles would hold equally true even in a one-paragraph assignment. Consider this example, a journal entry in which a student discusses the proverb, "Look Before You Leap":

> Like all well-known proverbs, "Look before you leap" expresses an obvious truth: that you shouldn't make quick decisions without full knowledge of the possible results. A good "real life" example would be what happened to my friend Pedro. With his last $3000 he bought a used car without bothering to have a mechanic check it first. Unfortunately, the car stopped running after a week, had to be towed, and has been parked in his driveway ever since. Obviously, he should have looked before he leaped.

As you can see, the topic sentence identifies the subject under consideration, the proverb in question. The support sentences explain the proverb's meaning and go on to describe an actual situation that illustrates the proverb's truth. The paragraph then concludes with a sentence that brings the reader back to the start by restating the proverb in slightly different wording. And adverbial transitions ("unfortunately" and "obviously") are used to facilitate the flow from idea to idea. This brings us to another consideration: the way in which the structure of a paragraph relates to the structure of the whole essay.

It would not be too much of an exaggeration to say that a paragraph can be seen as a mini-essay. Just as an essay begins with an introduction in which the thesis statement appears, a paragraph opens similarly, with a topic statement. And just as an essay develops its thesis through a series of body paragraphs, a paragraph develops its topic through a series of support sentences. Just as paragraphs sometimes open with helpful transitions, the sentences within paragraphs sometimes do as well. And just as an essay ends with a concluding paragraph, a paragraph ends with a concluding sentence. This makes sense because all writing—regardless of length—is attempting to do the same thing: Communicate with the reader. And this beginning/middle/end structure is usually what works best.

CONCLUSIONS

An essay's conclusion is just as important as its introduction. While the introduction constitutes the "first impression" the writer makes on the reader, the conclusion is what that reader comes away with. So if the essay ends poorly, what's gone before is undercut, diminished. Don't let that happen. Instead, end strong.

Always sum up in your last paragraph, which should begin with a re-phrasing of your thesis statement. In effect, the conclusion should resemble a *reversed* version of your introduction (although not word-for-word). Like an airplane rolling smoothly to a stop on the runway after reaching its destination rather than simply crashing there, the essay should close gracefully. This is easier to accomplish if you have used any of the introductory strategies explained earlier. You can simply revisit the scenario, statistic/fact, or quotation you opened with, thereby achieving a satisfying sense of closure by bringing the essay full-circle.

At several points now this book has mentioned the reader's psychology, a factor that any good writer bears always in mind. Conclusions are another example. People do not like to be driven out of town and stranded there. They much prefer to be chauffeured back home at the end of the day. In a sense, a good conclusion does that, by returning the reader to familiar turf. Accordingly, you should never introduce new ideas in your conclusion. Stick only to what's already been covered.

Let's look again at the revised introduction and conclusion of the "Million Dollar" essay. Notice how much they have in common. Several ideas introduced at the start are revisited at the end. (These have been underlined here for the sake of emphasis.)

Introduction

Most people have probably fantasized about what they'd do if they suddenly inherited a million dollars or <u>won it in a lottery</u>. Have you ever imagined yourself <u>being that lucky</u>? I know I have, many times. It will probably never happen, but I know what I'd do if it did. I'd make the absolute most of my <u>windfall, spending it wisely.</u>

Conclusion

So that's how I'd handle <u>my good luck</u>. Other people might spend their <u>windfall</u> differently, throwing wild parties or globe-trotting to the Caribbean, but not me. I'd prefer to react to my good fortune more cautiously, getting out of debt, making a few wise investments, taking a short trip to New York, buying a nice but not extravagant house and a new car, and helping out my loved ones and my church. Now that I've written my essay, I think I'll visit my neighborhood convenience store and <u>buy a lottery ticket</u>!

EXERCISES

1. Here are a half-dozen essay titles. Some are effective, but others are not. How might the ineffective ones be improved?

   ▶ The Lincoln and Kennedy Assassinations

   _____

   ▶ ISIS

   _____

   ▶ The Five Main Causes of the French & Indian War

   _____

   ▶ The Differences Between Neurosis and Psychosis

   _____

   ▶ Asperger's Syndrome and Attention Deficit Disorder

   _____

   ▶ My Proudest Moment

   _____

2. Select one of the *effective* essay titles in Exercise 1 and write an introduction paragraph based upon it. Make sure there's a firm thesis statement.

3. Here are five thought-provoking quotations. Choose three and write a good introductory paragraph based on each. Be sure that each paragraph ends with a firm thesis statement that echoes the quotation's wisdom (or lack of it), but in your own words.

   ▶ When you find you're on the side of the majority, it's time to reform. (Mark Twain)
   ▶ Poverty is the parent of revolution and crime. (Aristotle)
   ▶ There is only one religion, though there are a hundred versions of it. (George Bernard Shaw)
   ▶ Half the people you know are below average. (George Carlin)
   ▶ All human errors stem from impatience. (Franz Kafka)

4. Using your college library's most recent edition of *The Statistical Abstract of the United States*, find five interesting statistics that might be useful in the introduction (or body) of an essay about income inequality.

5. Using the "Look Before You Leap" paragraph on page 45 as a model, write similar paragraphs based on three of these other well-known proverbs. In each case, explain the proverb's meaning, and then describe an actual situation that illustrates the proverb's truth.

   ► A chain is only as strong as its weakest link.
   ► The early bird catches the worm.
   ► People who live in glass houses shouldn't throw stones.
   ► You can't judge a book by its cover.
   ► A leopard doesn't change its spots.

CHAPTER 6

Rewriting

LEARNING OBJECTIVES

When you complete this chapter, you will be able to

- ▶ Edit your writing to detect and correct problems with content, organization, style, and tone
- ▶ Proofread your writing to detect and correct typos and mechanical errors in spelling, punctuation, and grammar
- ▶ Develop peer reviewing skills that will enable you to assist classmates and benefit from their feedback in return

EDITING

Reportedly, the famous American author Ernest Hemingway spent ten days revising the last three paragraphs of his 1940 novel *For Whom the Bell Tolls*. While no professor would expect that level of commitment from a student in a first-year composition class, you *must* rewrite (and more than once) to achieve satisfactory results. This is because nobody produces good writing on the first try. The former United States Poet Laureate Billy Collins has said that we fine-tune using both a big screwdriver and a little screwdriver. The big one is for editing, fixing problems with regard to content, organization, style, and tone. Once these larger issues have been addressed, it's time to take out the little screwdriver and use it while proofreading to correct typos and "mechanical" errors, careless slip-ups in spelling, punctuation, and grammar.

Most writers do at least a little editing and fine-tuning even while drafting. They commit an obvious error and they fix it right away. Or perhaps they realize that a particular sentence is awkwardly constructed, so they revise it before moving on. But it's unwise to get bogged down making numerous corrections while attempting to create a first draft, because the interruptions necessitated by revising can derail your train of thought. Although some minor tweaking is inevitable along the way, in general it's better to concentrate first on completing the initial draft and postpone most polishing until later.

The editing stage of the writing process involves correcting problems with content, organization, style, and tone. Editing for content is quite difficult, however, because when writing you already know what you mean. If you didn't, you wouldn't be able to write at all. But what may be obvious to you as the writer may not be self-evident to the reader. So you must momentarily step outside yourself while editing and pretend to be that reader—someone who does *not* already know what the writing is all about. Granted, this reader-impersonation is not easy and may be only partially successful. Still, it's likely to reveal at least some points that need clarification or further development. What may have seemed logical or sufficient at the drafting stage might now strike you as much less so. You might want to add something here and there or take something out.

Very importantly, how about organization? Is everything where it belongs? Consider: CTA does not spell CAT. Although this may seem almost comically obvious, it can remind us of a basic principle about writing: Just as there's one and only one best location for every letter in a word, organization is crucial at every level—not only within words, but within sentences, paragraphs, and longer pieces of writing. So you must always ask yourself,

- ▶ Are the individual words in each sentence precisely the right ones and is each exactly where it belongs?
- ▶ Are the sentences in each paragraph presented in the best possible order?
- ▶ Are the paragraphs arranged in the best sequence?

In addition, look for ways to tighten your style. Try to adhere to the following principles, which are discussed in Appendix A:

- ▶ create active sentences with subjects and verbs side by side
- ▶ position modifiers near what they modify
- ▶ use transitions effectively
- ▶ handle numbers correctly
- ▶ use familiar vocabulary—nothing fancy
- ▶ write short sentences
- ▶ edit for concision and economy

While it's important to cultivate a style that avoids wordiness by expressing ideas as simply and directly as possible, it's equally necessary to ensure that your tone is appropriate to your purpose and your reader. Revisit Chapter 3, which discusses this while focusing on the need for reader-centered, positive wording that's sensitive to connotation as well as gender bias and other kinds of offensive expression.

PROOFREADING

This last stage of the rewriting process is the least creative, but it's extremely important. Your writing may be thoughtful, well-developed, well-organized, and fully appropriate with regard to style and tone. But if it's marred by keyboarding miscues and careless blunders in spelling, punctuation, and grammar, your credibility will be severely compromised. Therefore, you must take the necessary time to check for surface errors of this nature. Of course, most word-processing software includes spell-checkers and other such devices, and Microsoft Word even highlights questionable constructions. Take full advantage of these features. But don't rely on them absolutely. There's no substitute for your own careful attention to detail, especially since electronic resources are not foolproof. Spell-checkers, for example, typically provide several possible alternatives when they detect a mistake. But it's risky to simply select the first word on the list. Frequently, it's not the right choice. Always consult your dictionary before replacing your misspelled word with the one at the top of the list. In some cases, the meaning of that first word is far removed from what you intended. This can cause misunderstanding and, in some cases, unintentionally comical effects.

Here are some strategies for effective proofreading:

- ▶ Don't rush. Force yourself to go slowly by using the cursor, examining one word at a time.
- ▶ Proofread three times, checking for one thing each time: spelling first, then punctuation, then grammar. Review the guidelines in Appendix B to refresh your memory about these matters.
- ▶ After proofing electronically, print out your work and proof it once again to discover anything that might have escaped your notice on the screen.
- ▶ Read your work aloud, taking notice of where you stumble. Usually those are weak spots, instances of awkward or unnatural expression that need to be revised.

PEER REVIEWING

We've all heard the old saying "Two heads are better than one," and in most contexts this proverb is certainly true. Therefore, it makes sense to get help from someone else when attempting to edit or proofread. Many teachers of college-level English devise in-class exercises that require peer collaboration on editing and proof-reading. Sometimes the procedure involves two students trading papers and providing written comments on each other's work. Another approach is to provide the whole class with copies of several students' papers and have everyone discuss them all. In both kinds of situation, writers usually receive a great deal of helpful feedback. But even if your instructor does not employ such practices, it makes sense to involve yourself in this kind of activity on your own because it nearly always results in better writing.

But peer reviewing can be tricky. If a math student writes 2 + 2 = 5 and someone else rejects that equation as incorrect, it would be incorrect no matter who wrote it, so the rejection cannot be taken personally. Writing, however, is quite different, because it *is* personal—very much so. For this reason, most of us tend to be somewhat defensive about it. We don't like anyone to tinker with our prose. We take it as an affront. In reality, however, this instinctively self-protective reaction is actually self-defeating, because nothing is more helpful to a writer than constructive, well-intentioned criticism. But effective peer-reviewing can occur only if the reviewer employs the right tone. If the criticism is perceived as arrogant or hostile, nothing will be achieved. So the reviewer should be careful to avoid giving that impression.

This does not mean, though, that the reviewer should praise inferior work or refrain from pointing out shortcomings. Such reluctance to identify weaknesses does the writer no good. But the reviewer should exer-cise tact and sensitivity, mentioning strengths before focusing on areas needing improvement. And when weaknesses are mentioned they should be described gently, in a considerate way, while still providing spe-cifics. For example, if the writer failed to include enough detail about some feature of the topic, it would be unhelpful to respond with remarks like, "I don't know what you're talking about. You're not giving me anywhere near enough information to understand what you're trying to say." A far better response would be something like, "This topic is such an interesting one that I'd like to hear about it in greater depth. Maybe more details would give me a better understanding of your perspective."

But what if the topic is really *not* interesting to you? In a case like that it's helpful to remember what the great American novelist Henry James once said, that we should grant writers their givens and evaluate them only on the basis of how well they perform within that context. Additionally, it's important not to let your personal feelings toward the writer color your responses to the work. It's tempting to be overly generous toward someone you like and overly critical towards someone you find irritating. But these tendencies must be resisted, because they invalidate the whole endeavor. In any case, you should focus on large issues first— content, organization, style, tone—before taking out your "little screwdriver." And resist the urge to actually rewrite. Simply provide thoughtful suggestions that will help the writer do that. In the process, you'll begin to develop editing skills that will enable you to improve your own work as well.

What follows are three versions of a student essay. In its original form, the paper has its strengths. For starters, it's well-developed and well-organized. And it's lively. But it also exhibits a great many weaknesses. Marred by typos, misspellings, and other mechanical errors, it's rather wordy and rambling. Even more dam-agingly, however, the student introduces unnecessary subject matter, lapses into offensive language, and often chooses other vocabulary that's too informal for academic writing. Additionally, both the title and the con-clusion are insufficient. The second version of the paper has been rewritten to correct the major weaknesses already identified, but not the mechanical miscues. Notice how careful proofreading of the second version has identified those mistakes, which are corrected in the final version. Although that final version is not *perfect* (no essay ever is!), it's far better than the original, thanks to re-writing.

Maybe the original version strikes you as more "real," more engaging. You may relate well to the student's everyday wording and you may be amused by the references to her various misadventures. Further, you may feel that she's been admirably honest and sharing in mentioning her family problems. If so, that's understand-able, but only up to a point. As explained in Part 1, we must always remember purpose, audience, and tone. Although this would be classified as an example of self-expressive writing, its main purpose should be to inform and persuade, not entertain—unless the assignment called for a humorous approach. So the student's unwise spending in the past, her excesses at State U., her problems with her parents, and her unexplained hostility toward her brother contribute nothing toward moving the essay forward. In fact, they distract. Sometimes we feel obliged to "put everything in" simply because it's the truth, but that's not necessarily a constructive impulse. A good writer includes only what's relevant.

Further, the student's audience here is her professor, who will almost certainly expect the somewhat higher level of formality achieved in the final version. Although we should try to keep our writing accessible by avoiding an *overly* elevated style, it's nevertheless true that academic writing does operate on a higher plane than routine conversation. While your writing should echo your voice, it should be your "best" voice: the one you might use in a job interview, for example, rather than the one used while hanging out in the student lounge with close friends.

"A Million Dollars"

Lots of people—pretty much everybody, in fact—*have* has probably fantasized about what they'd

do if they suddenly inherited a million dollar*s* or won it in a lottery or something like that. Have

you ever imagined yourself being that lucky? I know I have, lots of times. It will probably never

happen, but I know what I'd do if it did. I'd make the absolute most of my windfall.

Before rushing out and squandering it all, I'd take care of business first. I have a lot of debt,

so I'd take care of that. My student loans would be first. Before coming to County *C*ommunity

*C*ollege I spent a semester at State U., where I *[slang]* partied my but off and flunked out. So I basically

wasted $8,000 in student loans. Since then I've *[slang]* racked up another *[spelling, slang]* coupla grand attending here. So

that's about $10,000 I'm *[slang]* in the hole for. I'd pay that off first. Then there's my charge cards. Don't

ask. When I got my first Master *C*ard back in high school I *[slang]* blew a bundle on a fancy watch for

this *[offensive term]* retard kid I was dating. We broke up after less than a year, but I was down more than *[slang]* 5 bens.

Then there were all these other stupid *[typo]* spendinmg sprees, so now the card's *[slang]* maxed out to the tune

of five G's. My Visa, too, is a disaster. I ran that one up after I could no longer use the *M*aster *C*ard.

Last year I went to Florida with my girlfriends on spring bre *[run-on]* ak, they had no money so I paid for a

lot of stuff. *[fragment]* More debt, three thou. After I paid all that off, *[I'd]* I'll invest in some stocks. G.E., Google *[spell out]*,

and Apple would be good bets. Of course, they could wind up being worthless, but *[I'd be]* I'm willing

to gamble because they *[would]* will probably continue to gain value, giving me interest income from

dividends in the future ~~after I've burned through my cool million~~.

After I cleaned up my financial mess, it would now be time to have some fun. Like *[many]* all girls,

[no caps] I LOVE to shop. Now I'd finally be able to buy all new clothes and *[spelling]* exsesserrys without having to

look at the price tags. But I wouldn't do my shopping around here, because all the stores here *[slang]* suck.

~~Me and~~ *M*y sister Jasmine, *[and I]* would take a weeklong trip to New York City and shop til we dropped.

We'd buy shoes, designer *[spelling]* jeens, tops, a *[spelling]* coupla new coats, purses, *[spelling]* jewerly, u name it. And while we

[spelling] was their we'd ~~do the whole tourist thing and~~ visit all the tourist attractions: Empire State Building,

[spelling] Stature of Loberty, *G*round *Z*ero, the Metropolitan Museum, *[and]* Central Park ~~and ect~~

My next big purchase would be my dream car—a red Mazda Miata. I've wanted one ever since I first saw it when visiting my aunt ~~in~~ *on* Cape Cod. There was one parked outside the restaurant where we ate one night and I said right then, "I've gotta have it!" My dream car would have a six-speed transmission and Pirelli racing tires. After getting my dream car I'd need someplace to live, because living with my parents really <u>sucks</u> *slang*, especially now because they've been <u>hassling me big time</u> *slang* ever since I flunked out of State. They act as if community college is some kind of disgrace. So I'd hire a contractor to build me a small place up in the mountains, Øn a <u>coupla</u> *spelling* acres of land, with central air *conditioning,* a fully equipped game room with bar, and a swimming pool.

I was complaining about my parents before, but really <u>their</u> *spelling* pretty cool, considering everything. So <u>wouldn't forget everything they</u> *they've* done for me over the years, so I <u>wouldn't forget</u> *avoid repetitious wording* them. I'd give them a hundred thousand out<u>right, may</u>be *run-on* that would make it a little easier for them to retire. They have always <u>worked their buts off</u> *slang* to support me and my sister, so they deserve it. I <u>ain't giving nothing</u> *grammer* to my brother, though. He <u>sucks</u> *slang*. Next would be my sister, Jasmine. She's <u>THE BEST</u>! *no caps* There's <u>Never</u> been a cooler <u>girl, she's</u> *run-on* like my best friend so she'd get $25 <u>thou</u> *slang* in addition to our New York <u>trip Next</u> *run-on* would be my church. I'm not <u>real</u> *very* religious but my whole family's been involved in a lot of church activities, so I'd give the church ten <u>grand</u> *slang* to fix up the social room and the black top in the parking <u>lot, it's</u> *run-on* in really rough shape.

So that's it. That's how I'd burn <u>threw</u> *spelling* my cool million!

There are several problems here.

First, the tone is much too informal and conversational. Avoid slang and overly casual expression.

Second, there are too many "mechanical" errors in spelling, punctuation, and grammar. Try to be more careful about those matters.

Third, your conclusion is much too "thin" and abrupt. Try to end more gracefully.

Please revise, paying attention to the corrections provided.

^xWhat I'd Do With A Million Dollars^x

Most people have
~~Lots of people—pretty much everybody, in fact—has~~ probably fantasized about what they'd do if they suddenly inherited a million dollar's or won it in a lottery ~~or something like that~~. Have you ever imagined yourself being that lucky? I know I have, *many* ~~lots of~~ times. It will probably never happen, but I know what I'd do if it did. I'd make the absolute most of my windfall.

~~Before rushing out and squandering it all,~~ I'd take care of business first. I have a lot of debt, so I'd take care of that. My student loans would be first. Before ~~coming to~~ *attending* County Community ~~*Avoid repetitious wording*~~ College I spent a semester at State U., where I neglected my studies and failed out, ~~So I~~ basically *wasting* wasted $8,000 ~~in student loans~~. Since then I've borrowed another $2,000 ~~to attend~~ *for tuition* here. So that's *start new paragraph* about $10,000 I owe. ~~I'd pay that off first.~~ *said this already* ~~Then there's~~ *Next would be* my charge cards. When I got my ~~first~~ Master Card back in high school I spent more than $500 on a fancy watch for a boy I was dating. ~~We broke up after less than a year, but I was down more than $500.~~ Then there were ~~all these~~ other stupid spending sprees, so now the card is at its limit of $5,000. My Visa, *card,* too, is a disaster. I ran that one up after I could no longer use the Master Card. Last year I went to Florida with my girlfriends on *run-on* spring break, they had no money so I ~~paid for~~ *covered* a lot of ~~stuff, amounting to~~ *our expenses, incurring more debt of* nearly $2,000. After I *$10,000* paid all that off, I'd invest in ~~some~~ stocks. General Electric, Google, and Apple would be good bets. Of course, they could wind up being worthless, but I'd be willing to gamble because they would probably continue to gain value, giving me ~~interest~~ income from dividends in the future.

After I cleaned up my financial mess, it would ~~now~~ be time to have some fun. Like many girls, I love to shop. Now I'd finally be able to buy all new clothes and *spelling* exsesserrys without having to look at the price tags. But I wouldn't do my shopping around here, because ~~all~~ the stores here *and I* are boring. ~~Me and~~ my sister ~~Jasmine~~ would take a weeklong shopping trip to New York City. We'd *spelling* *spelling* *were spelling* buy shoes, designer jeens, tops, coats, purses, and jewerly. And while we was their we'd visit all the *spelling* tourist attractions: the Empire State Building, the Stature of Liberty, Ground Zero, the Metropolitan Museum, and Central Park.

My next big purchase would be my dream car—a red Mazda Miata. I've wanted one ever since I first saw it when visiting my aunt on Cape Cod. There was one parked outside the restaurant where we ate one night and I said right then, "I've gotta have it!" My ~~dream car~~ would have a *[Avoid repetitious wording]*

Miata

six-speed transmission and Pirelli racing tires. After getting my ~~dream car~~ I'd need someplace to

live, because living with my parents is unpleasant, especially now because they've been critcizing

me ever since I flunked out of State. They act as if community college is some kind of disgrace. So

house   *spelling*

I'd hire a contractor to build me a small <u>place</u> up in the mountains, on a <u>coupla</u> of acres of land,

conditioning,

with central air, a fully equipped game room with bar, and a swimming pool.

spelling

I was complaining about my parents before, but really <u>their</u> pretty cool, considering

all they've   *said this already*

everything. So I wouldn't forget ~~everything they~~ done for me over the years, ~~so I wouldn't forget~~

$100,000   *run-on*

~~them~~. I'd give them ~~a hundred thousand~~ out<u>right, ma</u>ybe that would make it a little easier for them

to retire. They have always worked hard to support me and my sister, so they deserve it. Next would

run-on   *really*

be my sister, Jasmine. She's the best! There's <u>N</u>ever been a cooler <u>girl, she's</u> <u>like</u> my best friend so

run-on

she'd get $25,000 in addition to our New York t<u>rip, nex</u>t would be my church. I'm not very religious

donate

but my whole family's been involved in a lot of church activities, so I'd ~~give the church~~ $10,000 to

renovate   *repave*   *run-on*

~~fix up~~ the social room and ~~the black top in~~ the parking <u>lot, it</u>'s in really rough shape.

spelling

So <u>that</u>'s how I'd handle my good luck. Other people might spend <u>there</u> windfall differently,

spelling

throwing wild <u>partys</u> or globe-trotting to the Caribbean, but not me. I'd prefer to react to my good

fortune more cautiously, getting out of debt, making a few wise investments, taking a short trip to

spelling

New York, buying a nice but not <u>extravagent</u> house and a new car, and helping out my loved <u>one's</u>

spelling

and my church. Now that I've written my essay, I think I'll visit my neighborhood <u>convience</u> store

spelling

and <u>by</u> a lottery ticket!

Better! Your conclusion, especially, is much improved.

Notice, though, how I've provided additional revisions to show you how to tighten the style, using fewer words to express the same ideas. In addition, I've pointed out the remaining misspellings, crossed out unnecessary content, and made a few other suggestions.

What I'd Do With A Million Dollars: Wise Choices

Most people have probably fantasized about what they'd do if they suddenly inherited a million dollars or won it in a lottery. Have you ever imagined yourself being that lucky? I know I have, many times. It will probably never happen, but I know what I'd do if it did. I'd make the absolute most of my windfall, spending it wisely.

First I'd take care of my debts, starting with my student loans. Before attending County Community College I misspent a semester at State University, where I neglected my studies and failed out, basically wasting $8,000. Since then I've borrowed another $2,000 for tuition here. So that's about $10,000 I owe.

Next would be my charge cards. When I got my Master Card in high school I spent more than $500 on a fancy wristwatch for a boy I was dating. Then there were other unwise spending sprees, so now the card is at its limit of $5,000. My Visa Card is also a disaster. I ran that one up after I could no longer use the Master Card. Last year I went to Florida with my girlfriends on spring break. They had no money so I covered a lot of our expenses, incurring more debt of nearly $2,000.

After I got out of debt, I'd invest $100,000 in stocks. The stock market is unpredictable, but General Electric, Google, and Apple would be relatively safe bets. Of course, they could wind up being worthless, but I'm willing to gamble because they will probably continue to gain value, giving me income from dividends in the future.

After I cleaned up my finances, it would now be time to have some fun. Like many girls, I love to shop. Now I'd be able to buy new clothes and accessories without having to look at the price tags. But I wouldn't do my shopping locally, because the stores here are boring. My sister and I would take a weeklong shopping trip to New York City. We'd buy shoes, designer jeans, tops, coats, purses, and jewelry. And while we were there we'd visit all the tourist attractions: the Empire State Building, the Statue of Liberty, Ground Zero, the Metropolitan Museum, and Central Park.

My next purchase would be my dream car—a red Mazda Miata. I've wanted one ever since I first saw it when visiting my aunt on Cape Cod. There was one parked outside the restaurant where we ate one night and I said right then, "I've gotta have it!" My dream car would have a six-speed transmission and Pirelli racing tires. After getting my Miata I'd need someplace to live, because living with my parents is unpleasant, because they've been criticizing me ever since I flunked out of State. They act as if community college is some kind of disgrace. So I'd hire a contractor to build me a small house up in the mountains, on a couple of acres of land, with central air conditioning, a game room, and a swimming pool.

I was complaining about my parents earlier, but really they're pretty cool, considering everything. So I wouldn't forget all they've done for me over the years. I'd give them $100,000. Maybe that would make it a little easier for them to retire. They have always worked hard, so they deserve it. Next would be my sister. There's never been a cooler girl. She's really my best friend, so she'd get $25,000 in addition to our New York trip. Next would be my church. I'm not very religious but my whole family's been involved in many church activities, so I'd donate $10,000 to renovate the social room and repave the parking lot.

So that's how I'd handle my good luck. Other people might spend their windfall differently, throwing wild parties or globe-trotting to the Caribbean, but not me. I'd prefer to react to my good fortune more cautiously, getting out of debt, making a few wise investments, taking a short trip to New York, buying a nice but not extravagant house and a new car, and helping out my loved ones and my church. Now that I've written my essay, I think I'll visit my neighborhood convenience store and buy a lottery ticket!

NOW you've got it!

You've achieved a more appropriate tone, corrected the mechanical errors, provided necessary paragraph-breaks, and created a satisfying conclusion that relates back to the Introduction.

Well done!

EXERCISES

1. The following paragraph (from a "My Angriest Moment" essay) needs a lot of rewriting. Fix it up, focusing on mechanics (spelling, punctuation, grammar) and tone.

   As soon as that iceball hit my drivers side window something inside me just sort of snapped. I was like, "Whoa! No way I'm gonna let that go without kicking some but. Without even thinking about it I threw a u-turn right in front of oncoming traffic and speeded down the street, everybody was honking and slaming on there breaks but I didn't give a crap. And when I saw this scumbag kid running I knew he was the one that thrown the iceball. I got a little bit passed him and pulled over and jumped out of the car and grabed him by the cote.

2. Closely examine two versions of a paper you've written recently. Create a chart that reflects the kinds of revisions you made to the original when creating the final version: changes in content, tone, organization, and mechanics. Subdivide the mechanics section into typos, spelling, punctuation, and grammar. The chart can then be used as a helpful guide when rewriting in the future, as it will highlight the areas in which you tend to make the most mistakes.

3. Look again at the "Million Dollar" essay. Which of its middle paragraphs is the least well-developed? Why? If you were the writer, how would you improve it?

4. Before submitting your next essay assignment, exchange papers with someone else in the class and provide helpful feedback to each other.

PART 3

The Essay as Argument

As already discussed, a well-structured essay opens with a meaningful, clearly stated thesis. Since by definition a thesis is an assertion—something to be defended and proven—it's not an overstatement to say that in a sense all essays are argumentative and persuasive in nature. As the American author Joan Didion once said, writing is "the act of saying *I*, of imposing yourself on other people, of saying *listen to me, see it my way, change your mind.*"

But the whole idea of arguing to persuade is a complex proposition. If your listener or reader already agrees with you, there's no need to argue. You'd be "preaching to the choir." If your audience is neutral or undecided about the issue, it's possible they're not especially interested in it. And if they're in disagreement with you, you'll probably have a hard time changing their minds no matter how convincingly you make your case. Our harshly polarized political climate illustrates this.

Nevertheless, the ability to present your position clearly and coherently is a valuable skill, if only to clarify your own thinking or perhaps nudge resistant readers toward a somewhat broader perspective. Further, a well-argued essay can convince receptive readers to adopt a particular stance or solution in response to a given situation or problem.

Of course, there are many ways to flesh out an argument. Part 3 will acquaint you with some of the essential features of argumentative writing and will also discuss seven basic modes of development commonly used in structuring college-level essays.

CHAPTER 7

Essential Features of Argument and Persuasion

LEARNING OBJECTIVES

When you complete this chapter, you will be able to

▶ Compose a persuasive essay that uses valid evidence to successfully defend a relevant thesis
▶ Acknowledge and refute opposing viewpoints
▶ Employ both inductive and deductive reasoning
▶ Avoid logical fallacies

EVIDENCE-BASED THESIS

Legitimately persuasive writing must be based on valid evidence. According to Aristotle, this is argumentation based on *logos*—that is, verifiable facts. An objective, third-person approach is the most effective narrative perspective for logos-based argument, especially when dealing with a resistive audience. For example, it's better to say, "Women should be able to assume combat roles in the military" rather than "*In my opinion, I think* women should be able to assume combat roles in the military," because every person's statements are obviously that individual's opinion or belief, so it goes without saying.

But Aristotle also identified two other modes of argument: those based on *ethos* and *pathos*. Ethos-based evidence relies on establishing the speaker or writer's credibility, sincerity, and good intentions, and is therefore best-suited to undecided audiences. Not surprisingly, ethos-based argumentation often does employ first-person rather than third-person narration. Pathos-based argumentation appeals to the reader's personal values and feelings, and is very effective when dealing with an already receptive audience. However, this style of argumentation runs the risk of veering into the "appeal to emotion" fallacy. More about that later.

Regardless of the narrative perspective employed, the introductory paragraph of a persuasive essay should identify the issue at hand and then provide a firm, unambiguous thesis statement that clearly identifies your position. The thesis can be phrased positively ("X is good") or negatively ("X is not good"), but the reader should have no doubt about the direction of the argument. As explained in Chapter 4, however, you should avoid phrasing the thesis statement too absolutely. Allow for exceptions. For example, instead of saying "X is *always* good (or not good)," say *often* or *usually*. In truth, most situations are not subject to "black and white" treatment. There's nearly always at least some grey involved. Accordingly, terms like *rarely* (instead of *never*), *ordinarily* (instead of *always*), and others reflect this complexity and therefore make your thesis statement more credible because less inflexible.

In addition, the thesis statement should not only establish your position on the issue, but should also provide the basic reason for that position. For example, consider the difference between this thesis statement and its more persuasive revision:

Thesis: Cremation of the dead is usually more practical than traditional burial.

Revised Thesis: Cremation of the dead is usually more practical than traditional burial, because sprawling cemeteries are a waste of needed space, especially in densely developed urban areas.

ACKNOWLEDGING AND REFUTING OPPOSING VIEWPOINTS

Because any controversial issue is by definition debatable, an excellent strategy is to acknowledge at least some of the opposition's most credible arguments and then refute them, perhaps by applying an *ethos*-based strategy, reminding your audience of your expertise. Again, this makes your own assertions appear more reasonable and considered—and therefore more persuasive. Indeed, you can even structure the entire essay this way, opening each body paragraph with an opposing argument and then showing why it's mistaken. But it's crucial to ensure that your side has the last word at every point along the way. (This is mentioned again in the Comparison/Contrast section of Chapter 8.)

The proofs you use to refute the opposition and bolster your own thesis can be in the form of facts, statistics, expert testimony (that is, quotes from qualified authorities on the subject), anecdotes, and the like. Importantly, your evidence must be relevant, representative, and current. Many writers and public speakers like to invoke *pathos* at the end of their remarks, driving the main point home by appealing to the audience's hopes, fears, and desires. For the sake of credibility in written arguments, though, the sources of all your information must be fully documented, within the text and on an MLA- or APA-style list of sources, as in the model essay at the end of this chapter.

INDUCTIVE AND DEDUCTIVE REASONING

Clearly, all meaningful argumentation must be grounded in logical reasoning. There are essentially two kinds: *inductive* and *deductive*.

Inductive reasoning proceeds from the specific to the general. As such, it's probability-based. For example, let's say that you eat an apple on ten different occasions and become ill every time. Each instance of illness is a specific case, but taken together those ten cases lead to a safe assumption—that you're probably allergic to apples. Deductive reasoning, however, operates the other way around, proceeding from the general to the specific. For example, if you know that all the members of a particular campus club have a tattoo of a platypus on their left biceps, and you meet a student who's a member of that club, you can reasonably assume there's a platypus tattoo on his left biceps.

This kind of reasoning can be expressed in the form of a *syllogism*, which operates as follows:

Major Premise: All new BMWs are expensive. (True.)
Minor Premise: Her new car is a BMW. (True.)
Conclusion: Her new car was expensive. (No-brainer; conclusion is clearly true.)

Of course, for the conclusion to be reliable, both premises must be true, as in the above example. Here's a syllogism in which the major premise is false, because too sweeping in its assertion.

Major Premise: All Republicans oppose gun control. (Untrue: Sweeping Generalization.)
Minor Premise: Senator Longwind is a Republican. (True.)
Conclusion: Senator Longwind opposes gun control. (Not necessarily true.)

However, a syllogism's conclusion can be unreliable even if both premises are *true*, as in this example:

Major Premise:	Saxophones are loud. (True.)
Minor Premise:	This musical instrument is loud. (True.)
Conclusion:	This musical instrument is a saxophone. (Not necessarily true.)

Clearly, the reason why this syllogism is faulty is that the instrument mentioned in the minor premise does not necessarily belong to the category (saxophones) identified in the major premise.

Obviously, syllogisms are tricky, requiring careful thinking in order to arrive at meaningful conclusions. But that's why they're valuable to anyone attempting to construct a well-reasoned, genuinely persuasive argument.

LOGICAL FALLACIES

Argumentation using pathos-based strategies can be highly persuasive, because our emotions often color our responses. The influential psychologist Abraham Maslow (1908–1970) formulated an extensive list of our physical and emotional needs. Here's a fairly comprehensive inventory of emotional needs, based partly on Maslow's theories:

- ▶ The need to feel safe from harm or embarrassment
- ▶ The need to feel financially secure
- ▶ The need for meaningful accomplishments
- ▶ The need for recognition, affection, and approval
- ▶ The need to fit in with others and have friends
- ▶ The need to stand apart and be an individual
- ▶ The need to advise and nurture
- ▶ The need *for* advice and nurturing
- ▶ The need for fun, adventure, and escape
- ▶ The need for romance and sexual satisfaction

To recognize how appeals to emotion can function to persuade, we need look no farther than the world of advertising. In ad after ad, the implied message is that the purchase of a particular product or service will result in the fulfillment of one or more of these basic emotional desires. However, there is nothing logical about this. The product or service that the ad is promoting will not *necessarily* provide the promised emotional reward. It may or it may not, because many variables are always at work. Therefore, the appeal to emotion is perhaps the most common example of *logical fallacy*—that is, flawed reasoning.

There are many different kinds of fallacies in addition to the appeal to emotion. Here are ten of the most common:

Ad Hominem: From the Latin phrase meaning "to the person," an attack on the individual rather than a response to the actual issue. Example: "Of course you're opposed to capital punishment—you're always wrong about everything."

Appeal to Questionable Authority: Basing an argument on the opinion of someone who's not necessarily well-informed about the subject. Example: "There's no such thing as global warming. My barber was just saying so yesterday."

Bandwagon Appeal: Everybody's doing it, so you should (jump on the bandwagon) too. Example: "Everybody else in the neighborhood is voting for Joe Schmo, so you should also."

Begging the Question: A thesis that's phrased as if the point in contention were already proven. Example: "All those murderous people who work at Planned Parenthood should be fired and made to get real jobs."

False Dilemma: The "either/or" fallacy. Example: "If you don't major in business in college, you'll be a failure later on."

Generalizing from the Particular: Sometimes called "hasty generalization," using one case to support a sweeping claim. Example: "Women don't know anything about sports. My sister's a perfect example."

Invalid Analogy: Comparing two things that are not actually parallel. Example: "When there's a Democrat in the White House, it's like when Hitler was in charge in Germany."

Post Hoc, Ergo Propter Hoc: From the Latin phrase meaning "after this, therefore because of this," an assumption that one thing caused another just because it happened first. Example: "My sister always drank a lot of coffee, so she got cancer."

Red Herring: Introducing an irrelevant assertion to distract attention from the real issue. Example: "There's no need to worry about corporate tax evasion as long as the labor unions keep ruining the country."

Slippery Slope: The argument that one event will automatically lead to a whole subsequent chain of undesired results. Example: "If County Community College bans smoking on campus, nobody will enroll, faculty and staff will quit, and the college will have to close."

Clearly, effective persuasion must avoid fallacies—statements that violate basic principles of logic. If your essay is guilty of any such flaws, your argument is immediately discredited.

MODEL ARGUMENTATIVE ESSAY

Physician-Assisted Death: A Basic Right

Let's say your elderly, widowed mother has been diagnosed with terminal cancer. She has only six months to live. Moreover, she's in terrible pain. She has repeatedly said she wants to die as soon as possible and be reunited with your father in the afterlife. The whole family supports her wishes. She asks her doctor to prescribe a lethal dose of medicine so she can die with dignity when she feels fully ready. But unless you live in Oregon, Washington, or Montana, this can't happen (Braddock). Everywhere else, physician-assisted death (PAD) is illegal. This makes no sense. Mentally competent persons with terminal illness should certainly be able to end their own life if they want to.

Opponents of PAD claim that a doctor who complies with such a request violates the Hippocratic oath which says, in part, "First, do no harm." But this argument depends on how we define "harm." To enable a suffering patient to escape a prolonged period of pointless suffering and inexorable physical and psychological deterioration is actually an act of mercy. The true harm is in preventing that escape. Because of our laws, therefore, doctors in all but three states are actually *required* to do harm, oath or no oath. (Nitschke)

A related objection is that PAD denies the sanctity of human life. But there's nothing more important in life than a person's freedom and autonomy. Indeed, countless wars have been fought to ensure such liberty. Conversely, there's absolutely nothing sacred or noble about simply wasting away, becoming a mere shell of one's true self, all the while enduring pain, indignity, and the loss of independence (Messerli). Besides, the emphasis on sanctity is essentially a product of religious traditions, and since our laws require separation of church and state, such essentially faith-based preoccupations should have no influence on legislation.

Then there's the claim that if PAD is legalized, it will lead to widespread abuses. Selfish relatives and cost-conscious health insurance providers will somehow coerce patients into ending their lives unnecessarily, the argument goes, and PAD will occur disproportionately among the poor, uneducated, and otherwise marginalized members of society. But this is an example of the "slippery slope" fallacy (Frey). Thanks to strictly enforced procedural rules, there is no evidence demonstrating that any such over-use has occurred in the three states (and several European countries) where the practice is permitted. (Ganzini)

Admittedly, any debate involving death is weighty by nature. People argue all the time about such practices as abortion and capital punishment. But PAD is different, because it can occur only if the person involved chooses it; it's not up to anyone else. As Derek Humphrey, president of ERGO, an Oregon-based advocacy group, says on his Web site, "every competent adult has the incontestable right to humankind's ultimate civil and personal liberty—the right to die in a manner and at a time of their own choosing." ("Liberty")

Works Cited

Braddock, Clarence H. "Physician Aid-in-Dying." *Ethics in Medicine: University of Washington School of Medicine.* www.washington.edu/bioethx. Accessed 13 April 2017.

Frey, R.G. "Slippery Slope to Legalized Murder." *Euthanasia.* www.pro.con.org. Accessed 13 April 2017.

Ganzini, Linda. "Social Groups at Risk of Abuse." *Euthanasia.* www.pro.con.org. Accessed 13 April 2017.

Humphry, Derek. "Liberty and Death: A manifesto concerning an individual's right to choose to die." *ERGO: Euthanasia Research and Guidance Organization.* Accessed 13 April 2017.

Messerli, Joe. "Should an incurably-ill patient be able to commit physician-assisted suicide?" *In a Nutshell.* www.balancedpolitics.org. Accessed 13 April 2017.

Nitschke, Philip. "Hippocratic Oath and Prohibition of Killing." *Euthanasia.* www.pro.con.org. Accessed 13 April 2017.

EXERCISES

1. Here are ten examples of persuasive writing. Identify which of Aristotle's three modes (*logos, ethos, pathos*) would be operating in each situation.

    ▶ Fund-raising letter to local residents, soliciting money for the town's Cub Scout troop.

    _____

    ▶ Mayoral candidate's campaign speech emphasizing her experience and other credentials.

    _____

    ▶ Letter to the editor, urging that a traffic light be installed at a particularly dangerous intersection.

    _____

    ▶ Magazine article outlining the scientific community's collective stance on the dangers of climate change.

    _____

    ▶ Job application letter highlighting the applicant's qualifications and potential value to the employer.

    _____

    ▶ Social worker's report citing specific reasons why a particular child should be placed in protective custody.

    _____

    ▶ A landscaping services company's advertisement emphasizing the company's highly qualified personnel and many years in business.

    _____

    ▶ A public service announcement reminding senior citizens to get flu shots.

    _____

    ▶ An advertisement detailing the capabilities of a new model of surveillance drone.

    _____

▶   A feasibility study exploring the advantages and disadvantages of closing a major downtown street and creating a pedestrian mall.

_____

2.   Two of these syllogisms are valid examples of deductive logic, but three are invalid. Identify which are which, and provide reasons for your decisions.

Major Premise: Heavy metal bands all use drugs.
Minor Premise: Josh plays bass in a heavy metal band.
Conclusion: Josh uses drugs.

Valid or Invalid? _____

_____

Major Premise: Aaron always does poorly in math courses.
Minor Premise: MA 201-Trigonometry is a math course.
Conclusion: Aaron will do poorly in MA201.

Valid or Invalid? _____

_____

Major Premise: Many basketball players are tall.
Minor Premise: LaTonya is tall.
Conclusion: LaTonya is a basketball player.

Valid or Invalid? _____

_____

Major Premise: Steam locomotives are large.
Minor Premise: This locomotive is large.
Conclusion: This is a steam locomotive.

Valid or Invalid? _____

_____

Major Premise: Our team rarely loses a home game.
Minor Premise: This weekend's game is at home.
Conclusion: Our team will probably win this weekend's game.

Valid or Invalid? _____

_____

3. Envision a beer advertisement depicting a group of attractive, well-dressed young men and women partying at a fancy nightclub and drinking the advertised brand. Identify at least three basic human needs targeted by such an ad.

_____

_____

4. Identify the logical fallacy at work in each of the following statements:

▶ Everybody is voting for Carlos in the Student Government election, so you should vote for him too.

_____

▶ If the United States government doesn't put a stop to immigration, pretty soon there won't be any native-born Americans here.

_____

▶ You're a liberal, so nothing you say can be trusted.

_____

▶ My baseball coach says there's no such thing as evolution, so that's good enough for me.

_____

▶ Don't ever buy a Ford Mustang. My cousin had one and it was a total lemon.

_____

▶ Drug addiction is just simple immorality, like cheating on a test.

_____

▶ All those thieves on welfare should be required to pay back all that money they've stolen from us honest, hard-working citizens.

_____

▶ To get ahead today you have to either know somebody or break the rules.

_____

▶ I'm not going to listen to country-western music anymore. Every time I spend more than a couple of hours at a bar where there's country-western music I always have a headache the next day.

_____

► Don't worry about getting cancer from smoking. Everybody has to die from something sooner or later.

5. Choose one of the following topics and write a well-argued, fully-developed persuasive essay of 500–750 words.

► Assault Rifles Should/Should Not Be Banned
► Big-Time College Athletes Should/Should Not Be Classified as Professionals
► Student Evaluations of Teaching Should/Should Not Be the Main Way Professors are Evaluated for Promotion and Tenure
► Marijuana Should/Should Not Be Legalized for Recreational Use
► Mixed Martial Arts Competition Should/Should Not Be Banned

CHAPTER 8

Modes of Development

LEARNING OBJECTIVES

When you complete this chapter, you will be able to

Compose persuasive essays using each of the following modes of development:

- ▶ Narration
- ▶ Definition
- ▶ Description
- ▶ Exemplification
- ▶ Comparison and Contrast
- ▶ Process Analysis
- ▶ Cause and Effect

As mentioned earlier, an argumentative essay must make its case as persuasively as possible, presenting convincing evidence in support of its thesis. But there are many ways—modes of development—in which this can be accomplished. In *narration*, for example, the writer defends the thesis by providing an account of an event or experience that demonstrates the validity of the thesis. Similarly, an essay employing *exemplification* as its principal mode of development would provide several cases—or one fully developed instance —to illustrate the point at issue.

In any event, the mode of development chosen should be the one best-suited to the thesis. For instance, an essay attempting to prove that a particular situation is the result of several factors would obviously be best served by the *cause and effect* approach. Likewise, an essay asserting that a particular procedure is important and easy to learn would almost certainly adopt the *process analysis* mode. Indeed, it would not be an exaggeration to say that in argumentative writing the thesis itself, as much as the writer, chooses the mode of development.

Narration

On the most basic level, a narration is simply a chronological account of a series of events, whether factual or fictional. By that definition, there are many kinds of narration-based writing: newspaper stories, accident reports, and novels, to name just a few. In college English courses, however, the most typical form of narration-based assignment is the autobiographical essay, an account of a personal experience. It can also be an account of an envisioned *future* experience, as in the "Million Dollar" essay in Part 2. Most college writing instruction begins with this kind of essay because it's the easiest, requiring few resources other than the writer's already-established knowledge of the events. But a narrative essay should not be merely a meandering exercise in self-expression for its own sake. Like any essay, a narration should make a meaningful, impactful point that will interest and maybe even enlighten the reader.

CONFLICT

To create an effective narrative essay, you must choose relevant subject matter that will enable you to get and hold the reader's attention. For this reason, a narrative involving conflict is always a good choice because there's usually something instructive about how that conflict was—or was not—resolved. Indeed, the outcome of the conflict should illustrate the validity of your thesis. In literature (nearly all fiction and drama, along with much poetry), authors routinely portray conflict because without it there is essentially no story. Conflict is explored in somewhat greater depth in Chapter 10. More briefly stated, however, there are several basic kinds of conflict, categorized as follows:

- ▶ **Individual vs. Self**: Sometimes called "inner conflict," this always involves a person trying to choose between competing impulses. At its simplest it's a "good vs. evil" situation, but sometimes the conflict is more complicated.
- ▶ **Individual vs. Individual**: Essentially the "good guy vs. bad guy" scenario, but the variations are virtually unlimited: In short, one person against another—or, collectively, "us vs. them."
- ▶ **Individual vs. Society**: The person in conflict with the group, refusing to accept the norms of a repressive or otherwise mistaken community.
- ▶ **Individual vs. Nature**: The person in conflict with the great natural forces: forest fire, tornado, flood, blizzard, earthquake, and the like.
- ▶ **Individual vs. Fate**: Sometimes called "Individual vs. God (or the gods)," this conflict nearly always operates to the individual's disadvantage, as might be expected. By definition, fate has the upper hand.

POINT OF VIEW

There are two main ways to handle point of view in a piece of narrative writing, as shown below:

First-Person: I did this, I did that.

Third-Person: He/She/It/They did this, He/She/It/They did that.

Some English teachers instruct students never to use first-person, because in most kinds of writing the more objective third-person approach is preferable. Autobiographical narration, however, is the exception. Indeed, it's essentially impossible to write about your own experience *without* saying "I." When writing autobiography you are a participant in the action—indeed, the main participant—rather than merely an observer reporting it.

Since autobiographical narration is based on the writer's experience, the tone should be natural and conversational—the voice you might use when actually telling the story to a friend. Even at its most casual, however, writing is always a bit more formal than speech, especially in the academic context. Therefore, you should minimize the use of slang and should certainly avoid any terms that may give offense: no profanities, for example, and absolutely no slurs of any kind. Notice how the original version of the "Million Dollar" essay in Part 2 was "cleaned up" to achieve a more acceptable tone in the final version.

ORGANIZATION AND DEVELOPMENT

In autobiographical narrative, chronological organization usually works best. For this reason, it's wise to create a step-by-step outline of the sequence of events before writing the essay. This will help you refresh your memory of what happened and present the details in the most accurate order. A chronological outline for the model essay at the end of this section might look like this:

> Failed math
> Was in bad frame of mind
> Found toy gun
> Aimed gun at old man
> Man drew own gun
> Man identified self as detective
> Detective scolded me
> Learned lesson

Notice, however, that the introduction to that essay sort of plunges right into the climax ("I pulled a gun on a police officer") *before* recounting the events that led up to that moment. Although this is clearly a violation of chronological order, it's highly effective because it grabs the reader's full attention. Anyone seeing that sentence will almost certainly want to know the whole story. Another twist is the *flashback*, by which the narrator interrupts the unfolding story to mention an earlier event that has now taken on new importance because of its ability to shed light on more-recent developments.

VERB TENSE

Whether adhering to a strictly chronological approach or not, you must use verb tense consistently throughout the story. Some writers prefer present tense because it conveys a greater sense of immediacy, as in this example based on the sample essay:

> Present: I should be in a good mood, but I'm not.

> Past: I should've been in a good mood, but I wasn't.

But the present-tense approach is not advisable, because it's quite difficult to sustain without accidentally lapsing into the more accustomed past-tense style of narrating. Stick to past tense, and never shift back and forth between past and present, as in this example:

> (Past)
> So when my friend Tom and I <u>were</u> aimlessly walking…

> (Present)
> the stage <u>is</u> set for trouble.

This is a very common error, and is extremely disruptive to the narrative flow. Make every effort to avoid it.

In addition, you should use chronology-based transition words and phrases a bit more than you might in actual conversation. Here are some useful ones that enable the reader to more easily follow the unfolding narrative.

after	last
as	later
at last	meanwhile
before	next
during	soon
eventually	suddenly
finally	then
first, second, third	while

SENSORY DETAIL

A good narrative provides enough specific details to enable the reader to "experience" the events. Especially helpful are details that relate to the senses: not only sight but also hearing, smell, taste, and touch. Notice, for example, the many descriptive words that appear in the sample essay: The night was *dark*, the handgun was *small*, the trash bag was a *big plastic* one, the *old* man was wearing a *suit and tie,* and so on. But you should resist the urge to tell every single thing about the experience simply because it happened. Instead, choose details selectively, including those that will help the reader follow, understand, and relate to the story. Discard the irrelevant. For example, in the revision of the "Million Dollar" essay in Part 2, the student's mention of her unexplained hostility toward her brother has been deleted because it's not pertinent to the discussion.

DIALOGUE

One effective way of moving a narrative forward is to have the characters in the story talk to each other, just as people do in real life. The technical term for such conversation is *dialogue.* It's important to use dialogue correctly, observing certain rules.

▶ To prevent confusion, always indicate who is speaking, like this:

> "How are you today?" he said.
> "Not so good," she said.
> "Why? What's the matter?" he said.

▶ Although "said" is the most common verb in such situations, it can become annoyingly repetitious if over-used. Note how this revision corrects that:

> "How are you today?" he asked.
> "Not so good," she replied.
> "Why? What's the matter?" he inquired.

▶ Remember that in real life people nearly always use contractions. Therefore, your dialogue should as well. For example, in the above exchange, "What's" is used rather than "What is."

▶ Providing "he said/she said" phrases is called *attribution*. Here are a dozen useful attribution verbs:

coaxed	muttered
demanded	responded
exclaimed	sobbed
explained	shouted
inquired	stammered
insisted	urged

Indeed, virtually any verb having to do with speaking can be used for attribution. But it's crucial to use the most appropriate attribution verb in each situation, because these words convey a lot about the characters and their interactions. To say "whispered," for example, when there's no reason for the person to be whispering would make no sense.

▶ Use quotation marks correctly, placing them only around the speaker's exact words, rather than around summary statements of what was said.

WRONG: He asked her, "how she was today."
RIGHT: He asked her, "How are you today?"

Notice that—as in the above examples—attribution sometimes appears before the quote, rather than after. It can also interrupt the quote, as in this example:

"Actually," she replied, "not so good."

CONCLUSION

A good autobiographical narrative should have an instructive message or lesson of some sort and that moral should emerge clearly. Although this point is sometimes stated—or at least implied—in the thesis statement in the introduction, it usually appears most forcefully in the conclusion, where the writer sums up. After the reader finishes, there should be no doubt about the writer's feelings toward the experience described. And if the narrative has been skillfully crafted, the reader should now share those sentiments. Ideally, the reader should have learned something about life or at least been reminded of a truth already known.

Like the "Million Dollar" paper in Part 2, the essay that follows is an example of first-person autobiographical narrative. It has an attention-getting introduction, is well developed with relevant details, makes effective use of dialogue, employs an engagingly colloquial style, and summarizes persuasively in the conclusion.

CHECKLIST: NARRATIVE ESSAY

A good narration-based essay

- ▶ Has a meaningful title that clearly identifies the topic

- ▶ Opens with an interesting, attention-getting introduction that establishes the significance of the topic, and provides a firm thesis statement

- ▶ Recounts something that has happened (often something involving conflict)

- ▶ Is organized into three or four body paragraphs, covering the topic in a coherent, step-by-step way, focusing on one main idea at a time, usually in chronological order

- ▶ Provides enough concrete, specific detail to enable the reader to envision the events of the narrative

- ▶ Employs dialogue to advance the story

- ▶ Closes with a smooth, meaningful conclusion that gracefully resolves the discussion by somehow relating back to the introduction

- ▶ Uses clear, simple, straightforward language—nothing fancy

- ▶ Maintains an appropriate tone, neither too formal nor too conversational

- ▶ Contains no inappropriate material

- ▶ Contains no typos or mechanical errors in spelling, capitalization, punctuation, or grammar

- ▶ Satisfies the length requirements of the assignment

MODEL NARRATIVE ESSAY

My Closest Call

Most of us have had a serious brush with danger at least once or twice, often during our teen years. If we're lucky, we survive the incident relatively unharmed and, after we've had time to think about it, come to understand what we've learned from the experience. That was certainly true in my case. My most dangerous moment was when I pulled a gun on a police officer.

Summer vacation had just started, right after my junior year of high school. I should've been in a good mood, but I wasn't. I'd just failed math and, in addition to the disappointment and very vocal disapproval of my parents, was facing nothing more enjoyable than summer school and the prospect of having to repeat the class as a senior if I flunked it again—a very real possibility. Needless to say, I was extremely frustrated, resentful, and angry. And at that point I didn't really care about anything very much.

So when my friend Tom and I were aimlessly walking around the neighborhood one dark night, looking for something exciting to do, the stage was set for trouble. As we passed a row of garbage cans, I was surprised to see a small handgun lying on top of a big plastic bag of trash. At least I thought it was a gun; really it was just a toy. But—made of dull black plastic—it looked very, very real. Right away I knew we could have some "fun" with it.

We kept walking, sort of playing with the gun, handing it back and forth, pretending to shoot each other and imaginary enemies. We were too old for this kind of nonsense, but we were getting a kick out of it anyway. Finally we got tired of the game and I put the gun in my back pocket. Just then we saw what appeared to be a slightly intoxicated old man wearing a suit and tie, shuffling toward us about twenty yards away. "Let's scare him," I said to Tom, who eagerly nodded his approval.

"Gimmie your wallet," I shouted at the man, pointing the gun at him menacingly. I wasn't intending to actually rob him, and I hadn't thought about how he might react, but what happened next turned out to be the most unexpected—and most dangerous—moment of my life. In one graceful, obviously much-practiced motion, he dodged to his left, went down on one knee, and had me in the sights of his own all-too-genuine pistol. "Police! Drop it! Drop it!" he bellowed. But I already had, and I was yelling now too: "Toy gun! Toy gun! Don't shoot!" He slowly rose, walked over to us, holstered his weapon, introduced himself as a plainclothes inspector, and calmly advised me, "Son, I almost put a bullet right between your eyes." My answer came out in a shaky squeak: "I'm glad you didn't." He replied, "So am I."

To my absolute astonishment, that was it. He didn't arrest us, didn't slap us around, didn't even ask for any identification. Just gave us a brief scolding and ordered us to go home and stay out of trouble. Of course, Tom told everybody in the neighborhood about what had happened, and as the story got passed around it got all distorted and blown out of proportion. So I became a mini-celebrity that summer, "the kid who shot it out with the state troopers in the middle of the night." But I wasn't enjoying the notoriety. Instead, I was thinking about how lucky I'd been, how incredibly no-sweat the detective had been, and how I'd never do anything that totally stupid, ever again.

Definition

One of the obvious reasons why speakers of a shared language are able to communicate is that words have specific, agreed-upon meanings. Sometimes, however, a word might be known to the speaker or writer but not to the listener or reader. Additionally, many words have more than one meaning. These complications can result in miscommunication and sometimes even angry disagreement. Therefore, it's often necessary to define our terms in order to prevent misunderstanding. But there are several kinds of definition, ranging from very simple to more developed.

KINDS OF DEFINITION

When we attempt to define, our topic is always predetermined by the situation at hand, and our reasons for addressing it—in short, our purpose and our audience. As in virtually all writing situations, these considerations will in turn dictate our approach. There are several kinds of definition, each serving a different kind of objective.

Synonym Definition

The most basic form of definition is the *synonym*, a word whose meaning is essentially the same as that of another word—the one being defined. This concept is well-known to anyone who enjoys crossword puzzles or has ever used a thesaurus—essentially a dictionary consisting entirely of synonyms. When using this type of definition, however, it's very important to choose a synonym that will be readily understood. If the synonym and the word or phrase being defined are equally unfamiliar, the definition is useless. For example, to define *coterminous* as *contiguous* would probably accomplish nothing because both words would be unknown to most readers.

Sentence Definition

At the next level is the *formal* or *sentence* definition, which follows a standard format: the term being defined, its class, and the features or characteristics that differentiate it from other members of that class. Conveniently, two such definitions appear above:

Term	Class	Differentiating Characteristics
synonym	word	whose meaning is…the same as…another
thesaurus	dictionary	consisting entirely of synonyms

Stipulative Definition

There is also the *stipulative* definition, which is necessary when a particular word or phrase is subject to multiple interpretations and the speaker or writer wishes to establish which of them applies in the given instance. For example, the term "well-qualified" means different things to different people, so a Human Resources director using that term should define it, perhaps like this: "We are seeking a well-qualified applicant, someone with a college degree and at least three years of experience."

As always, audience analysis is crucial. Someone writing about military service, for example, would have to clearly define any acronyms or terms unique to that environment unless the intended reader(s) also had experience in the armed forces. When uncertain about such matters, it's always best to err on the side of caution. Avoid jargon (specialized or technical language of a particular profession or group) unless you are sure it will be understood, and provide brief parenthetical definitions of any terms that might be unfamiliar. Notice, for example, how the term "jargon" has been clarified here.

Extended Definition

Most challenging is the *extended* definition, an in-depth, essay-length treatment of the term, expression, or concept under consideration. Because on its own it's rather "thin" and uninteresting, extended definition is nearly always used in conjunction with other rhetorical strategies such as description, exemplification, cause and effect, and so on. For instance, the model essay at the end of this section discusses schizophrenia by employing not only definition but also descriptions and examples of specific behaviors throughout. In addition, the essay uses cause and effect, specifying how those actions result in various undesirable outcomes. Thanks to these features, the essay is successful in making its point that schizophrenia is a multifaceted diagnosis, important to pin down precisely.

When employing such approaches to help develop an extended definition, it's best to rank-order and present the examples and other details in "important/more important/most important" sequence. As explained in Chapter 4, this ascending order is always best because it positions the most interesting or convincing material near the end, thereby giving the essay greater forward momentum.

DEFINITION AND PERSUASION

Although the primary purpose of definition is to inform and clarify, extended definition nearly always functions in support of a thesis. As mentioned earlier, the writer might be applying spin, casting the subject in a new light, perhaps to encourage the reader to re-think it. Clearly, the most useful purpose of definition is to persuade.

Let's consider the legal term "plea bargaining," which Barron's *Law Dictionary* defines objectively as "the process whereby the accused and the prosecutor negotiate a mutually satisfactory disposition of the case." But plea bargaining has its opponents, many of whom might define it rather differently in order to discredit it.

For example, Albert Alschuler, Professor Emeritus of Law at Northwestern University and longtime critic of plea bargaining, has provided this definition: "A perfectly designed system to produce convictions of the innocent." Indeed, Alschuler's version served as the basis of a well-argued condemnation of the practice during a 2004 PBS *Frontline* interview. But his definition, while perhaps accurate, is obviously not objective. Still, absolute objectivity is difficult if not impossible to achieve. Even the above dictionary definition could be challenged on the basis that the word "satisfactory" is open to interpretation.

RESEARCH-BASED DEFINITION

In many cases a definition can be derived from observed evidence. An essay about zydeco, for example, might define it simply as "lively, upbeat, accordion-based folk music." Other situations, however, may require a higher level of technical detail. This is extremely difficult—indeed, impossible—unless the writer possesses the necessary knowledge. If not, research must come into play. For example, the *Merriam-Webster* online dictionary defines *zydeco* as "popular music of southern Louisiana that combines tunes of French origin with elements of Caribbean music and the blues and that features guitar, washboard, and accordion." In such cases you must somehow acknowledge the sources of your information, preferably by using a standard system of documentation. In English classes, the Modern Language Association (MLA) style is required. The following model essay, for example, includes parenthetical citations within the text and a correctly formatted "Works Cited" page crediting the paper's sources.

CHECKLIST: DEFINITION ESSAY

A good definition-based essay

- ► Has a meaningful title that clearly identifies the topic

- ► Opens with an interesting, attention-getting introduction that establishes the significance of the term, expression, or concept that will be defined, and provides a firm thesis statement

- ► Is organized into three or four body paragraphs, covering the topic in a coherent, step-by-step way, focusing on one main idea at a time, in logical sequence

- ► Provides enough concrete, specific detail to fully develop the ideas, using examples, descriptions, and other modes of development to clarify the definition

- ► Closes with a smooth, meaningful conclusion that gracefully resolves the discussion by somehow relating back to the introduction

- ► Uses clear, simple, straightforward language—nothing fancy

- ► Maintains an appropriate tone, neither too formal nor too conversational

- ► Contains no inappropriate material

- ► Contains no typos or mechanical errors in spelling, capitalization, punctuation, or grammar

- ► Satisfies the length requirements of the assignment

MODEL DEFINITION ESSAY

Schizophrenia: What Is It?

In the field of abnormal psychology, there are many identifiable conditions that have by now been studied and clearly labeled. Of these, schizophrenia is among the most well-known. Basically, schizophrenia can be defined as a chronic form of psychosis that causes the misinterpretation of reality, resulting in behavioral irregularities. But it's not simply one disorder. Rather, there are a number of variations, all related but distinct (Miller 3). As explained on the Mayo Clinic's Web page on the subject, there are three major kinds of schizophrenia: paranoid, catatonic, and disorganized. For purposes of treatment, it's important to understand the differences among these. (Schizophrenia)

Catatonic schizophrenia is a psychosis that causes the sufferer's conduct to veer from one end of the behavioral spectrum to the other. The person may experience episodes of total immobility, entering a nearly catatonic state in which all ability to communicate or even move is suspended. But the person may also become extremely hyperactive, excitedly pacing, twitching, or flailing around for no apparent reason, grimacing or gesturing inappropriately, or repeatedly mimicking other people's words or movements (Rosa). Clearly, catatonic schizophrenia is extremely disruptive to normal functioning.

Paranoid schizophrenia is a psychosis that causes the sufferer to lose touch with actuality and develop delusional beliefs. Such persons sometimes "hear things" and nearly always imagine that someone is "out to get them." They manage to function reasonably well in everyday situations, but their far-fetched ideas create a range of problems. For example, the paranoid schizophrenic might suffer from anxiety and anger, and may become violent if the delusions are dismissed or ridiculed by others. At the very least, the person's comments typically cause others to disassociate, and the person's consequent emotional isolation and generalized unhappiness and can even lead to suicide. ("Paranoid")

Also known as hebephrenic schizophrenia, disorganized schizophrenia is yet another chronic form of psychosis. The worst kind of schizophrenia, it causes the sufferer to exhibit behaviors that greatly interfere with normal living, because the person's thoughts, words, and actions often follow no logical pattern. As a result, the person may be quite unable to function independently, having no ability to perform necessary activities such as bathing, cooking, getting dressed, and the like. In addition, the person might babble, laugh inappropriately, or even become combative. (Carey)

Clearly, schizophrenia in all its forms is a major problem. Fortunately, however, it is relatively manageable today, thanks to a various medications that can be prescribed. But drugs are only one component of treatment. The patient's treatment plan may also include psychotherapy, psychosocial therapy, electroconvulsive therapy, and—in crisis situations—hospitalization, as well as additional features such as family therapy and vocational training. Treatment teams may also include psychologists, social workers, psychiatric nurses, and a case manager who coordinates the effort ("Schizophrenia"). For any of this to be effective, however, there must first be an accurate diagnosis of what kind of schizophrenia is present.

Works Cited

Carey, Benedict. "Schizophrenia—Disorganized Type." *New York Times*. www.health.nytimes.com. Accessed 10 Feb. 2017.

Miller, Rachel, editor. *Diagnosis: Schizophrenia*. Columbia UP, 2002.

"Paranoid Schizophrenia." *CNN Health*. www.cnn.com/health. Accessed 10 Feb. 2016.

Rosa, Matthew H., M.D. "What is Catatonic Schizophrenia? What Causes Catatonic Schizophrenia?" *Medical News Today*. www.medicalnewstoday.com. Accessed 10 Feb. 2017.

"Schizophrenia: Treatments and Drugs." *Mayo Clinic*. www.mayoclinic.com. Accessed 10 Feb. 2017.

Description

The purpose of description is to provide the reader with a vivid mental picture of the subject: the person, place, or thing described. This is done by including specific details that capture the subject's physical characteristics. Writing instructors often assign an essay whose whole purpose is to describe. However, effective description will energize any essay, allowing the subject—and the writer's attitude toward it—to emerge more clearly. Accordingly, good description not only enables the reader to experience what's being described, but also creates an overall impression of it. Hence, description is a highly effective means of persuasion.

POINT OF VIEW

A description-based essay can employ either first-person or third-person point of view. The choice is determined by the essay's topic and purpose. For example, the writer of the model essay at the end of this section is describing her own room, and is attempting to demonstrate that, as her thesis says, "this room...suits my purposes perfectly." Therefore, she uses first-person point of view. To do otherwise would make little sense in this context.

But in other instances, third-person point of view might be the better choice. For example, this description of upright pianos is entirely objective, with no personal dimension:

> Upright pianos are sometimes called vertical pianos because, although their keyboards look the same as those of grand pianos, their inner workings are perpendicular to the floor. Less expensive than grand pianos and only a few feet wide (as opposed to the five-to-nine feet of grand pianos), they take up much less space and can be found in homes, schools, and bars. Their only real weakness is that their sound quality is not as impressive as that of grand pianos. There are basically three kinds of uprights: the spinet, the console, and the studio. These vary primarily in size; the spinet is about three feet high, the console is a few inches higher, and the studio ranges from about forty-five to fifty inches. There's also the upright player piano, very popular during the early twentieth century but not often seen today. It's really just a gimmick, and requires no actual musicianship. The music is produced automatically by a kind of music box mechanism inside.

Even the seemingly judgmental comments about player pianos are based on verifiable facts with which no musician would disagree. Therefore, third-person point of view is consistently maintained—and fully appropriate—in this paragraph.

ORGANIZATION AND DEVELOPMENT

Good description is well organized, providing details in logical sequence. If the purpose is to describe a personal experience, as in the sample narrative essay that appears earlier in this chapter, *chronological* order is nearly always the best approach, facilitated by the use of transitions. But if the purpose is to describe a place or thing, *spatial* order is usually the appropriate choice. Correct spatial order is partly determined by the writer's vantage point—that is, whether the writer is observing and reporting from a fixed position or is describing while on the move. It's usually better to write descriptions from a fixed vantage point, because this approach makes the organization easier to control. The writer can describe the subject by sequencing the details in a systematic way—from top to bottom, perhaps, or from left to right. Such description often uses special transition words such as the following:

above	in
alongside	inside
behind	near
below	on
between	outside
beyond	under

Notice, for example, how the model descriptive essay at the end of this section uses a fixed vantage point (from the doorway of the room) and uses spatial transitions (*inside, beneath, between,* and others) to describe the room and its furnishings in an orderly way.

SENSORY DETAIL

Our perceptions of physical reality are provided by our five senses: sight, hearing, smell, taste, and touch. Like narration, effective description relies on these. Indeed, it would be impossible to describe anything without stating what it looked like, sounded like, and so forth. While sensory impact is crucial to good descriptive writing, selectivity and specificity are just as important. Rather than burdening the reader with *unnecessary* description, the essay should focus on what's relevant—those key details that will best enable the reader to fully experience the subject. And those details should be expressed concretely rather than in general terms. Simile and metaphor can be quite useful in this context. For example, the phrase "an acrid, skunk-like stench" gives the reader far more information than simply "a bad smell." Here are other examples of bland, unhelpful description followed by revisions enlivened by key sensory details:

SIGHT: He was big

    Revision: He was well over 6′1″ and weighed more than 250 pounds.

SOUND: The machine was making a loud noise.

    Revision: The machine was producing a high-pitched, screeching whine like the noise caused by a loose fan belt.

TASTE: The dessert tasted good.

    Revision: The dessert had a sweet, peachy flavor.

TOUCH: The shirt felt nice.

    Revision: The shirt had a smooth, silky texture.

SUBJECTIVE AND OBJECTIVE DESCRIPTION

When describing a person or a concept, neither chronological nor spatial organization really applies. In those situations, writers sequence the details according to relative importance (usually moving from least to most significant) or from general details to more-specific ones. Of course, this kind of sequencing depends on the writer's judgment about those distinctions. This brings us to the differences between *subjective description* and *objective description*.

Imagine that you have been asked to write two paragraphs: first, a straightforward description of a barn; second, a description of how that same barn might appear to you if you knew that a murder had been committed there. Such an assignment would be certain to produce two very contrasting treatments of the subject. The first paragraph would be observation-based, mentioning the barn's size, color, and other readily noticeable features. Factual and dispassionate, it would probably not differ too greatly from someone else's description of the barn. In short, it would be an example of *objective description*. But the second paragraph would be colored by your awareness of the crime. The barn would not have changed, but you would be seeing it differently now. Hence the resulting description would probably be quite dissimilar from the earlier version. Influenced by personal feelings, it would be an example of *subjective description*.

USING DESCRIPTION TO PERSUADE

Because subjective description is governed by the writer's own attitudes toward the subject, subjective description primarily seeks to influence—unlike objective description, which primarily seeks to inform. But this is more complicated than it seems; most description is a blend of the two. Notice, for instance, that in the model narrative essay, the writer says that his toy pistol "looked very, very real." This is a subjective judgment, but he supports it by providing the objective detail that it was "made of dull black plastic." And when he describes the detective as "a slightly intoxicated old man wearing a suit and tie," the first part of that description is subjective (and perhaps inaccurate) while the mention of the man's clothing is objective. Clearly, subjective and objective description can function in support of each other. But, like a narrative essay or a definition essay, a descriptive essay should not be merely an exercise for its own sake. Rather, it should serve a larger purpose—to convey the dominant impression or controlling idea identified in its introduction. Description usually functions in the service of an essay's thesis.

In the sample descriptive essay at the end of this section, for example, the student plainly states in her introduction that she considers her room ideal for her current circumstances: "this room…suits my purposes perfectly." She then uses an abundance of objective description to reinforce that subjective thesis. The many details that follow in the body paragraphs all serve to support her claim. Notice that the organization of the essay is quite disciplined. She begins by establishing the physical characteristics of the room: its size and shape, the locations and features of windows and doors, and its technical components (heat, lighting, electrical outlets). From there she goes on to describe the décor and furnishings, and finally she describes the personal belongings that make the room recognizably her own. Whether you're writing description or anything else, always strive for that level of orderliness.

CHECKLIST: DESCRIPTIVE ESSAY

A good description-based essay

- ► Has a meaningful title that clearly identifies the topic

- ► Opens with an interesting, attention-getting introduction that establishes the significance of the person, place, or thing that will be described, and provides a firm thesis statement

- ► Is organized into three or four body paragraphs, covering the subject in a coherent, step-by-step way, focusing on one main idea at a time, in logical sequence

- ► Provides enough concrete, sensory detail to convey a vivid mental image of the subject

- ► Achieves balance between subjective and objective description

- ► Closes with a smooth, satisfying conclusion that gracefully resolves the discussion by somehow relating back to the introduction

- ► Uses clear, simple, straightforward language—nothing fancy

- ► Maintains an appropriate tone, neither too formal nor too conversational

- ► Contains no inappropriate material

- ► Contains no typos or mechanical errors in spelling, capitalization, punctuation, or grammar

- ► Satisfies the length requirements of the assignment

MODEL DESCRIPTIVE ESSAY

My Room: A Home Away From Home

When I enrolled at County Community College, I had to find suitable living arrangements somewhere nearby. Luckily, I was able to rent a comfortable furnished room in a relatively crime-free neighborhood within walking distance of campus, in a house owned by Mrs. Greene, an elderly widow. This has turned out to be an excellent arrangement. I have kitchen privileges, my own bathroom, and very reasonable rent. In return, I'm supposed to keep my room and bathroom clean, help with household chores like mowing the lawn, shoveling snow, and dragging the garbage can out to the curb every week. That's fine with me, because Mrs. Greene needs the assistance and I need this room, which suits my purposes perfectly.

Located just inside the back door of the house and right next to my bathroom, the room is fairly small, no more than fifteen feet square, but it has a ten-foot ceiling that makes it feel bigger. In addition to my door, which is equipped with a lock, there are three windows that make the room bright and airy, two on the wall that's to your right when you enter and one on the wall directly in front of you. All three windows are covered by adjustable white venetian blinds and there's a heat vent beneath each of them. There's an oval ceiling light and several convenient electrical outlets built into the baseboards. Strangely, there's no closet, but there are three coat-hooks on the back of the door and that's all I really need because I don't have a lot of clothing. The room is painted beige, with white woodwork.

As I said, the room is furnished, and it has light brown wall-to-wall carpeting. My bed, covered with a red blanket, is against the left-hand (windowless) wall. The window in the wall straight ahead of you is surrounded on all sides by built-in, floor-to-ceiling bookcases painted white. There's a comfortable tan corduroy easy chair in the right corner, with a floor lamp behind it. Between the two windows in the right-hand wall is a brown, six-drawer bureau. There's a large wooden desk and matching chair positioned on the last wall, to the right of the door as you enter.

There's plenty of room for my belongings. In fact, I use some of the bookshelves for storing shoes, sweaters, and other clothing, along with my textbooks and other school supplies. Also on the shelves are six trophies I've won in local running races, and my three favorite stuffed animals. I have a few decorations on the walls: my high school diploma, a framed photo of my parents and brother, and a framed poster of the late Grete Waitz, a famous marathoner who has always been an inspiration to me. Hanging from a hook is my old field hockey stick. Although I no longer play that sport, seeing the stick brings back many great high school memories. I have to admit that the desk is pretty cluttered, holding not only a lamp, an alarm clock, and my computer, but piles of books, magazines, and school-related papers, along with a stapler and a college mug containing pens, pencils, a small ruler, a letter opener, and a pair of scissors.

Nobody could ever accuse me of living the lifestyle of the rich and famous, but for now this room is all I need. It's safe, affordable, adequately furnished, conveniently located, and large enough for my needs, and I'm lucky to have found it. Moreover, Mrs. Greene and I have become good friends, so I expect to be here until I graduate.

Exemplification

Sometimes called *illustration*, this essay development strategy supports and clarifies the thesis statement by providing specific examples that move the essay forward, beyond mere generalization. In short, the thesis statement tells the reader what the essay is about, but the examples *show*, taking the discussion from the abstract to the concrete and preventing pointless repetition. Examples can reinforce an easily understood thesis (e.g., "a longer school day will not actually improve student performance"), but can also be used to illustrate difficult or unfamiliar concepts (e.g., "economy of scale"). In either case, examples must always be accurate, relevant, and interesting. Among the most common kinds are statistics, pertinent facts, anecdotal evidence, and expert opinion.

Of course, examples should be lively and engaging, to ensure that the reader will remain interested in the discussion. Therefore, highly technical examples should be avoided, unless the intended reader can be assumed to possess the knowledge or training necessary to understand such references. This is true whether exemplification is the essay's governing approach or not. If the topic of any essay requires specialized examples, they must be clarified in layperson's terms. Notice, for instance, how the model definition-based essay that appears earlier in this chapter accommodates the uninitiated reader. The three categories of schizophrenia—catatonic, paranoid, and hebephrenic—are illustrated by plainly-worded examples of specific behaviors typical of each.

POINT OF VIEW

Like most kinds of writing, exemplification-based essays ordinarily employ third-person point of view. There's usually nothing to be gained by using the subjective first-person approach when presenting factual information. The one exception to this would be an essay in which exemplification were used to discuss the writer's personal experiences in support of the thesis. An example might be an essay in which the writer challenges the concept of gender stereotypes and provides three or four examples of personal friends who transcend those broad assumptions. Of course, most essays of any kind seek to argue a point and provide support for the writer's personal opinions, as in the model essay at the end of this section. Notice how that essay employs a blend of first- and third-person narration to achieve its purposes.

ORGANIZATION AND DEVELOPMENT

Unless your approach to the topic requires a chronological handling, examples should be presented in ascending order of importance, with the most compelling examples appearing last. But an exemplification-based essay can be organized in several other ways as well:

- ▶ It can build on one specific example that's mentioned within the thesis statement. The body paragraphs of the essay would then provide sub-examples—examples of the example, so to speak. Such a thesis statement might look something like this: "Although good food is fundamental to a restaurant's success, other factors are also crucial; the wait staff, for example, can make or break an establishment." The essay would then go on to provide examples of good and bad service.
- ▶ A more common strategy, however, is to proceed from a broader thesis statement and then provide varied illustrations of that generalization. An essay seeking to defend the thesis that athletic stardom does not necessarily make someone a worthy role model could be supported by a series of one-paragraph discussions of individual athletes' bad behavior. This is the approach used in the model essay at the end of this section.

RESEARCH-BASED EXEMPLIFICATION

Any thesis statement is essentially an expression of the writer's opinion. To defend your thesis—especially if it's controversial—it's sometimes advisable to go beyond personal experience and provide authoritative examples more likely to convince the reader. Therefore, it may be necessary to conduct research, drawing upon statistics, case studies, expert opinion, and the like. Although an exemplification essay need not become a full-blown research project, there's nothing wrong with using quotation, paraphrase, or other supporting details from reputable sources to reinforce your position. As always when using outside sources, documentation is required.

To serve their purpose, examples must be typical and *representative*, rather than unusual or outlying. A quote from a scientist who's a global warming denier, for instance, would be unpersuasive because the scientific community is nearly unanimous in recognizing the dangers of climate change. But an NRA spokesperson's condemnation of gun control legislation would be a valid example, because that large and influential organization strongly opposes such restrictions. For that matter, such a statement could even operate in reverse, serving as a *negative* example in an essay attempting to discredit the NRA's position. Genuinely representative examples can be used with equal effectiveness to bolster opposing viewpoints on the same issue. Of course, the way in which examples are used—positively or negatively—will depend on the essay's thesis.

CHECKLIST: EXEMPLIFICATION ESSAY

A good example-based essay

- ▶ Has a meaningful title that clearly identifies the topic

- ▶ Opens with an interesting, attention-getting introduction that again identifies the topic, establishes its significance, and provides a firm thesis statement

- ▶ Is organized into three or four body paragraphs, covering the topic in a coherent, step-by-step way, focusing on one main idea at a time, progressing from the abstract to the concrete

- ▶ Provides enough typical, representative examples to fully support the thesis

- ▶ Organizes support in ascending order of importance

- ▶ Closes with a smooth, satisfying conclusion that gracefully resolves the discussion by somehow relating back to the introduction

- ▶ Uses clear, simple, straightforward language—nothing fancy

- ▶ Maintains an appropriate tone, neither too formal nor too conversational

- ▶ Contains no inappropriate material

- ▶ Contains no typos or mechanical errors in spelling, capitalization, punctuation, or grammar

- ▶ Satisfies the length requirements of the assignment

MODEL EXEMPLIFICATION ESSAY

Conversationalists from Hell

The basic theme of French philosopher Jean Paul Sartre's famous 1944 play "No Exit" can be summed up rather concisely: Hell is other people. Fortunately, most of us would be reluctant to adopt such a dreary perspective. Indeed, it's a given that our most meaningful experiences in life derive from our relationships with others. Sometimes, however, I'm tempted to suspect that Sartre was actually onto something— especially when I encounter certain particularly irritating habits among people with whom I must interact.

For example, there are certain individuals who simply do not understand the concept of the "rhetorical question." You must never say "Hi! How are you?" when encountering these folks, because you'll be required to stand there for at least a half an hour, nodding with feigned commiseration while being regaled with a seemingly endless catalog of complaints, grievances, and generalized whining. This is especially tiresome if the tale of woe involves medical difficulties. Social norms require such bellyaching to be received sympathetically, even when we suspect that the malady is being exaggerated, or—worse—if we've heard it all before. If only they'd they just lie and say, "Fine, thanks. And you?"

In a similar vein, there are those intensely annoying characters who feel obliged to "one-up" whomever they're conversing with, especially at the workplace lunch table or break room. If you happen to mention that your cousin just won a Mercedes Benz in a raffle, there's always the co-worker who will counter with an anecdote about *his* cousin, who just won a full-sized, working replica of the Starship Enterprise. You know it's absolute nonsense, in part because you've seen this act before (repeatedly!). And it's insulting because the implication is that you're gullible enough to swallow such malarkey. But again, social norms prevent you from calling him out. That would be giving him too much importance. Besides, what if—just this once—he's telling the truth? So you're exasperated once again.

Perhaps my pet peeve, however, involves people who have no sense of phone etiquette. There are few experiences more deeply aggravating than to engage in conversation with one of these knuckleheads, and realize that you're involved in unwitting competition with their mobile device. They're talking to you, yes, but all the while glancing down at incoming text messages, giving you—at best—half their attention. This maddening gaffe is so widespread that it was the subject of a December 2015 Doonesbury cartoon, in which the title character actually walks away from his wife, who continues to text, not even realizing he's gone. A comic strip, but all too real.

What all three of these examples have in common is a basic lack of consideration. It might also be seen as simple arrogance, the underlying belief that other people's needs must take a back seat to our own. When that kind of dynamic is at work, it's tempting to embrace Sartre's pessimistic message. Luckily, however, the behaviors discussed here are still exceptions rather than norms, so we need not despair—tempting though it can sometimes seem when confronted with boorish conduct.

Comparison and Contrast

In everyday life we often compare and contrast in order to make routine decisions. At lunch, for example, we might be torn between the healthful salad and the "heart attack special." The same is true of large, life-altering choices; when selecting a college, a job, or even a mate, we must evaluate the available options. Of course, the lunchtime scenario involves a quick, "on the fly" (perhaps even subconscious) decision, while these other examples would require true deliberation. Indeed, in the latter context it's advisable to actually write down a list of the similarities and differences of the two or more competing alternatives in order to identify their relative advantages and disadvantages—in other words, to conduct a cost/benefit analysis. It would be unwise not to, because it's important to organize our thoughts. Certainly this is equally true when attempting to compose a comparison/contrast essay in response to an assignment.

This kind of essay explores similarities and/or differences between two related subjects in order to shed light on both, and—often—to demonstrate that one is preferable to the other. Another common purpose is to show that two subjects that seem very different are actually similar, or vice-versa. Accordingly, the introduction must identify the two subjects, indicate that they will be compared and/or contrasted, and provide a firm thesis statement that reflects the essay's larger purpose and intentions. Ideally, the essay will go beyond the obvious, pointing out similarities and/or differences that are not immediately apparent. And, to be convincing, the essay should focus on at least three shared characteristics of the two subjects.

POINT OF VIEW

A biology test might require you to compare and contrast DNA and RNA; an art exam might require you to discuss contrasting features of early and late Renaissance painting; a history exam might ask you to discuss how the contrasting approaches of Malcolm X and Martin Luther King served their common objectives. In each case, the subjects under consideration are related to each other in some meaningful way, belonging to the same class or category. If they weren't, the whole exercise would be pointless or even absurd. It's possible to compare a peach and a pear, because both are foods—specifically, fruit. But it would be silly to compare a peach and a pork chop; although both are foods, they belong to entirely different categories of food, rendering comparison meaningless. The subjects must share a fundamental basis of similarity, upon which a treatment of their differences can be built. Otherwise, it becomes impossible to devise a worthwhile thesis—a controlling idea that gives the essay its direction.

The thesis in a comparison/contrast essay should not simply state the obvious fact that the two subjects are alike and/or different. It must go a step further, establishing why these parallel features are meaningful. Here's an example of a weak (because self-evident) thesis, coupled with a revised version that identifies the real point:

> Weak Thesis: Los Angeles and San Francisco are the two most important cities in California, but they are very different.
>
> Revision: The differences between Los Angeles and San Francisco clearly reflect the contrasting histories of California's two most important cities.

Notice, however, that in comparison/contrast essays—as in most kinds of writing—the purpose is to defend a position, make a point. Therefore, the objective third-person point of view is again preferable to subjective first-person narration.

ORGANIZATION AND DEVELOPMENT

If you're experiencing difficulty formulating a thesis, you might not have devoted enough time to pre-writing. For example, creating lists of the similarities and differences between the two subjects will enable you to determine the three or four most *significant* ways in which they're alike or different, and this can lead you to your real point. One interesting strategy is to play *devil's advocate* (presenting a viewpoint that contradicts the consensus). If the subjects are basically alike, you may want to focus on the most important way in which they differ. Conversely, if they are clearly dissimilar, you may want to find the most relevant point of similarity. Here are examples of both kinds of thesis.

> The laptop computer and the iPad are essentially alike, performing many of the same functions. But the latter has at least one distinct advantage; its much smaller size makes it lighter and therefore more conveniently portable.

> Although Ezra Pound and T. S. Eliot were very different poets, they did share one characteristic in addition to their considerable fame: a deplorable strain of anti-Semitism that must negatively affect our estimate of both.

Sometimes your list-making will reveal that there are actually more similarities than you'd originally supposed, or more differences. Such a discovery can be troubling, because now you're fighting an uphill battle. The solution? Simply adjust your thesis, reversing it in response to this new evidence. This kind of situation is another illustration of the fact that writing helps us clarify our own thinking.

SUBJECT-BASED STRUCTURE VS. CHARACTERISTIC-BASED STRUCTURE

A comparison/contrast essay can be structured in either of two ways. The discussion can begin by dealing with the first subject and its characteristics and then move on to deal with the second subject and its parallel characteristics. This approach is a bit unwieldy, however, because it results in an essay with two fairly lengthy "middle" paragraphs rather than the customary three or four. In effect, it becomes two mini-essays spliced together. Additionally, it requires the reader to hold in memory everything that's been said about the first subject while reading about the second.

On the other hand, this can actually work to your advantage if you're deliberately trying to discredit the first subject in order to promote the second. Nevertheless, a more typical approach is to discuss one *characteristic* at a time. The following chart, which represents a hypothetical essay discussing two baseball teams, illustrates the two differing approaches.

Approach # 1 (Subject-Based)	**Approach # 2 (Characteristic-Based)**
Introduction	Introduction
Team A—fielding, hitting, pitching	Fielding—Team A & Team B
Team B—fielding, hitting, pitching	Hitting—Team A & Team B
Conclusion	Pitching—Team A & Team B
	Conclusion

When using Approach #2, it's appropriate to deal with both similarities and differences when discussing each characteristic. The paragraph about pitching, for example, might develop like this:

> Both teams have deep pitching staffs, with both right-handed and left-handed hurlers, and both teams have two effective relief pitchers. In addition, both pitching staffs are relatively young, averaging about twenty-five years of age. But statistics reveal that during the past three seasons Team B's lefties have a far lower earned-run average than Team A's, and Team B's relief pitchers have recorded more saves. In addition, Team B's pitching coach is far more respected than Team A's; in fact, he's considered one of the best in the game. Clearly, Team B has the advantage when it comes to pitching.

As shown on the previous page, the essay should deal with the same three or four characteristics for each subject. Importantly, these characteristics must be relevant and meaningful. It would be pointless, for example, to discuss the similarities and/or differences between the two teams' uniforms, because these would in no way influence the teams' performance. In addition, the characteristics of the two subjects should be covered in the same sequence, moving from simplest to most complex. This ensures that the discussion will be balanced in its treatment of the two subjects, thereby avoiding the appearance of bias.

TRANSITIONS

As mentioned throughout this book, transitions are very helpful. Chronologically oriented transitions appear in narrative writing and spatial transitions in descriptive writing. Since comparison/contrast is by its very nature directly concerned with similarities and differences, this kind of essay benefits greatly from the use of transitions that relate accordingly. Words and expressions like *and, similarly,* and *likewise* (to reinforce similarity) and *but, conversely, on the contrary,* and *on the other hand* (to reinforce difference) and others go a long way toward conveying the points being made. Notice how transitions (underlined) function in this paragraph.

> The lead guitar and the bass guitar are similar in some respects. Both are electrified string instruments fundamental to jazz, rock, and other kinds of popular music. <u>On the other hand</u>, they are quite different in a number of ways. The lead guitar has a fretted neck, while the bass guitar's neck is sometimes fretless. With its six strings, the lead guitar can produce a broad range of notes. <u>Conversely</u>, the bass guitar's four heavier strings produce only lowernotes, as the instrument's name reflects. The dominant lead guitar appears to stand apart, independent. <u>But</u> this is an illusion. The unobtrusive bass plays an equally important role, interacting with the drums to provide a supportive foundation on which the lead very much depends.

SIMILE, METAPHOR, ANALOGY

When using comparison/contrast, whether as an end in itself or in the service of some other strategy, *similes* and *metaphors* are quite helpful in clarifying the subject matter. Basically, simile involves a comparison using the words "like" or "as." Metaphor, on the other hand, does not use those words, and simply equates the two things being compared, often by using some form of the verb "to be" (is, are, was, were, will be).

Simile: "Float like a butterfly, sting like a bee" (Mohammed Ali)

Metaphor: "All the world's a stage" (Shakespeare)

Analogy is yet another creative form of comparison. Basically an extended simile or metaphor, it typically compares one thing to another in order to illustrate or dramatize the latter of the two, enabling the reader to better envision it. The names of many tools and similar devices are essentially analogies; think *claw* hammer, *C* clamp, and *T* square. In the sports world, analogies abound. In football we have the *blitz* and the *Hail Mary*, in baseball the *stolen* base and the *double-header*, in basketball the *travelling* violation and the *stutter-step*. In the same way, we employ analogy when we speak of an *avalanche* of data, a *tsunami* of bad news, a *landslide* election victory, or a legal decision that *opens the floodgates*. But analogies can be far more developed than these compact terms. Here's an example.

> The student who becomes entrapped in a poorly-taught online course faces the same predicament as Kafka's hapless, groping protagonists in his novels *The Castle* and *The Trial*. Despite their best efforts, those characters cannot determine what's expected of them, and wholesale confusion results. In much the same way, the frustrated student lacks clear directions or regular, constructive feedback from the instructor, and must operate on instinct, relying largely on guesswork when attempting to satisfy course requirements.

USING COMPARISON AND CONTRAST TO PERSUADE

Since your purpose in a comparison/contrast essay is usually to persuade the reader that one subject is superior to another, it makes sense to give "your" subject the advantage of having the last word by always discussing it second. This was mentioned in Chapter 7 and illustrated by the baseball example provided earlier in this chapter. Team B has a clear advantage because in both approaches its characteristics can function in refutation or contradiction of Team A's. Coupled with third-person point of view, this is a very effective strategy.

CHECKLIST: COMPARISON/CONTRAST ESSAY

A good comparison/contrast-based essay

- ▶ Has a meaningful title that clearly identifies the topic

- ▶ Opens with an interesting, attention-getting introduction that again identifies the topic, clearly reveals whether the essay will focus on similarities or differences, and provides a firm thesis statement

- ▶ Is organized into three or four body paragraphs, covering the topic in a coherent, step-by-step way, focusing on one main idea at a time, in logical sequence

- ▶ Employs either a subject-based or characteristic-based approach

- ▶ Provides enough concrete, specific detail to fully develop the ideas (perhaps using simile, metaphor, or analogy)

- ▶ Closes with a smooth, satisfying conclusion that gracefully resolves the discussion by somehow relating back to the introduction

- ▶ Uses clear, simple, straightforward language—nothing fancy

- ▶ Maintains an appropriate tone, neither too formal nor too conversational

- ▶ Contains no inappropriate material

- ▶ Contains no typos or mechanical errors in spelling, capitalization, punctuation, or grammar

- ▶ Satisfies the length requirements of the assignment

MODEL COMPARISON/CONTRAST ESSAY

Rover and Kitty: The Odd Couple

Of all the household pets, dogs and cats are certainly the most common. And although many people own at least one of each, it's typical to prefer one species over the other. This is understandable because—despite their obvious similarities—dogs and cats are very different animals. Dogs, for example, say "Bow Wow," while cats say "Meow Meow." But the contrasts go far beyond their vocabularies.

For starters, dogs are territorial and protective. If a stranger (or even the letter carrier) comes to your door, the dog will immediately announce himself, barking and maybe even snarling, as if to say, "This is OUR house! Keep your hands where I can see them and don't try any funny business." The cat, on the other hand, will probably ignore the person's arrival, or perhaps scurry away and fall asleep under the sofa. There are advantages and disadvantages to both behaviors. While most dogs will protect you from intruders, their frequent barking and howling can annoy the neighbors and become a real nuisance. Worse, dogs have been known to attack for little reason. Ever notice how many are muzzled? Conversely, the cat is no help in a crisis, but her quiet, understated demeanor makes her less likely to become an aggravation, and she's surely not a danger to anyone. She'll never get you sued.

Dogs crave attention, and need a lot of tender, loving care. Among other things, this involves training, to moderate their naturally rambunctious and destructive tendencies. They must be taught manners and self-control. This can take a lot of time and effort, and requires a great deal of patience. Unfortunately, many dog owners neglect this responsibility and wind up with a canine felon on their hands. And—for obvious reasons—even well-trained, perfectly behaved pups still need to be walked, sometimes very early in the morning…in all weather. Training the cat? Forget about it. She'll sharpen her nails on the upholstery no matter what you do to discourage her. But she's aloof and independent, requiring nothing much more than a couple of square meals a day and a clean litter box. She comes and goes as she pleases, and as long as she doesn't get run over by a car, that's that.

As for companionship, the differences are again apparent. The dog gives constant feedback, panting excitedly, jumping about, and enthusiastically agreeing to practically any kind of game. He'll shake hands, roll over, play dead. He'll chase a stick, he'll swim with you, and he loves to go out for a run. True, most kittens also like to goof around, but the adult cat withholds affection. She'll rub against your leg, sit in your lap, and purr contentedly when petted—but only when she's in the mood. In short, she calls the shots. It's her ball, her gym, her game.

Bottom line? Pet ownership is like most things in life. There are trade-offs. The dopey dog is high maintenance, but he'll reward you more generously. The clever cat doesn't ask for much at all, but she owns you, rather than the other way around. Maybe that's the cat's appeal. We love our dogs, but we continue to accommodate and pamper our cats because on some level we suspect they may actually be smarter than we are.

Process Analysis

There are two kinds of process analysis: informational and instructive. Informational process analysis clarifies how something happens. An example would be an explanation of how rust forms or how soil erosion occurs. Clearly, the purpose of such writing is not to enable the reader to perform the process, but simply to understand it. Instructive process analysis, on the other hand, does explain how to perform a particular procedure. An example would be an essay about how to apply the Heimlich maneuver or negotiate the purchase of a new car. In college writing classes, process analysis assignments are usually instructive in nature. Accordingly, this section focuses primarily on that kind of process analysis.

PROCESS ANALYSIS IN RELATION TO OTHER MODES

Clearly, process analysis is related to other kinds of essay development. It resembles narrative, for example, because it's chronological. It often involves definition and/or description because—depending on the procedure being explained—certain terms and objects might have to be identified. And process is always related to cause and effect because the whole purpose of following those steps is to ensure a desired outcome. Perhaps most importantly, process analysis can certainly function to persuade, as in an anti-hazing essay deploring what a fraternity pledge must endure when subjected to demeaning and dangerous initiation rituals. Similarly, an instructive process analysis essay outlining healthy pre-natal practices can serve to encourage responsible behavior by expectant mothers. Clearly, process analysis can be a highly effective tool of persuasion.

POINT OF VIEW

Like any other essay, a process analysis paper should open with an effective introduction that provides a thesis—a firm statement not only of what the reader will learn how to do, but also why it's worthwhile to know. Consider these examples:

> **Thesis:** When using Microsoft Word to create a document, it's important to know how to move text from one location to another.

> **Revised Thesis:** When using Microsoft Word to create a document, it's important to know how to move text from one location to another, because the ability to "cut and paste" will enable you to avoid unnecessary re-typing.

Notice, however, that this revised thesis uses the word "you," as if the writer were actually addressing the reader in conversation. This is the most effective narrative approach to employ in process analysis. But it's not first-person point of view, because the emphasis should be on the reader rather than the writer. Therefore, the word "I" should not appear. Like most kinds of writing, then, process analysis uses third-person point of view, but with the kind of reader-centered perspective discussed in Chapter 3.

ORGANIZATION AND DEVELOPMENT

In addition to providing necessary context and establishing the thesis, the introduction (or perhaps the first body paragraph) should identify any required tools or other equipment. The body paragraphs of the essay should then walk the reader through the procedure, following a logical, step-by-step chronology and providing all pertinent details, presented in the form of simple, active commands, like this: "Push the red button, then push the blue button." But if two actions must be performed simultaneously, they should be combined. For example, instead of saying, "Push the blue lever forward. Before releasing the blue lever, push the red button," say this: "While holding the blue lever forward, push the red button."

And, for the sake of both convenience and safety, it's important to alert the reader to anything that might go wrong, and provide "troubleshooting" suggestions about how to prevent or solve such problems, as in the following paragraph about operating a gasoline-powered snow thrower.

> If the machine begins to vibrate excessively, there may be loose parts or a damaged auger. Stop the engine immediately, disconnect the spark plug wire, and tighten all nuts and bolts. Reconnect the spark plug wire and restart the engine. If the vibration continues, have the machine serviced by a qualified technician.

Although logical organization is a fundamental requirement of all writing, it's especially crucial in process analysis because the steps involved in most procedures must be performed in order, with no deviation. Perhaps more than any other kind of essay, therefore, process analysis requires extensive pre-writing exercises, to guarantee that nothing is left out or mis-sequenced. A good way to test the sequencing of your process analysis is to observe while someone unfamiliar with the procedure attempts to perform it while reading your essay. But for this test to be valid, you must resist the temptation to provide assistance if the person hesitates or expresses uncertainty. This will enable you to detect problems and revise accordingly. Another effective test is to ask someone who *is* familiar with the procedure to critique your essay. Even better, subject your essay to both forms of evaluation.

TRANSITIONS

In process analysis, transition words and phrases are especially helpful in clarifying the relationships among the steps in the procedure. Terms like "first," "next," "then," and "finally" are quite helpful to the reader. What's not helpful, however, is the adoption of what might be called "recipe style," in which short words like "a" and "the" are left out.

The omission of such words creates a choppy, disjointed effect that actually interferes with the reader's comprehension. Notice the differences between these two explanations of how to control the temperature of a two-burner electric hot plate.

> **Original:** Use control knobs to adjust temperature of heating coils. Turn knobs clockwise to raise temperature, counter-clockwise to lower temperature.

> **Revision:** Use the control knobs to adjust the temperature of the heating coils. Turn the knobs clockwise to raise the temperature, counter-clockwise to lower the temperature.

We sometimes talk about people's ability to envision things in their "mind's eye," but it's equally important to consider the "mind's ear" because readers mentally "hear" as they process text. For this reason, the more conventional phrasing of the above revision is preferable to the original.

CHECKLIST: PROCESS ANALYSIS ESSAY

A good process analysis-based essay

▶ Has a meaningful title that clearly identifies the topic

▶ Opens with an interesting, attention-getting introduction that again identifies the topic, establishes why the procedure is important to master, and provides a firm thesis statement

▶ Identifies all necessary equipment, tools, and materials

▶ Is organized into three or four body paragraphs, covering the topic in a coherent, step-by-step way, focusing on one main idea at a time, in chronological sequence

▶ Provides enough concrete, specific detail to fully explain the procedure

▶ Closes with a smooth, satisfying conclusion that gracefully resolves the discussion by somehow relating back to the introduction

▶ Uses clear, simple, straightforward language—nothing fancy

▶ Maintains an appropriate tone, neither too formal nor too conversational

▶ Contains no inappropriate material

▶ Contains no typos or mechanical errors in spelling, capitalization, punctuation, or grammar

▶ Satisfies the length requirements of the assignment

MODEL PROCESS ANALYSIS ESSAY

How to Change a Flat Tire

Nearly every motorist experiences a flat tire sooner or later. Therefore, you should be prepared for such a situation. To change a tire you'll need the following items, which should be carried in your trunk at all times: at least six flares, a properly-inflated spare tire, a lug wrench, a wide wooden board, and a jack. Changing a flat is fairly simple, but the correct procedure must be followed to prevent injury or vehicle damage.

As soon as you realize you're developing a flat, drive the car onto the road shoulder. Park as far from the road as you can, and on as flat and level a surface as possible. Activate the warning flashers, put the transmission in park, set the emergency brake, and turn off the engine. If your car has a standard transmission, put it in reverse. Open the trunk and set up the flares behind and in front of the car as a signal to other drivers.

Remove the spare and other equipment from the trunk. If your lug nuts are visible, you're ready to proceed. But if they're hidden by a hub cap, use the jack handle to pry it off. Using the lug wrench, fully loosen—but do not remove—the nuts by turning them counter-clockwise. If they're reverse-threaded and must therefore be turned clockwise, there will be an "L" on each lug bolt. Removal of the lug nuts is the only difficult part of the task, because it requires some physical strength. A very long-handled lug wrench is helpful, because it provides greater leverage. A common practice is to use your foot to push down on the wrench handle.

Since there are several kinds of jacks, consult your owner's manual for proper assembly and use, and then position the jack. If the ground is soft, put the wooden board under the jack base to stabilize it. Jack up the car until the flat is just clear of the ground, and remove the jack handle. The handle should always be removed when you're not using it, because this prevents you from accidentally knocking into it and dislodging the jack—a dangerous error. Remove the lug nuts by hand and put them into your pocket or into the hubcap for safekeeping. Remove the flat. Roll the spare into position and put it on the wheel by aligning the holes in the rim with the lug bolts on the wheel. You may have to jack the vehicle up a bit more to accomplish this, as the properly inflated spare will be fatter than the flat and will therefore require more ground clearance. Holding the spare firmly against the wheel with one hand, use your other hand to manually replace the lug nuts as tightly as possible. Do *not* use the wrench.

Lower the car back down. Now you may use the wrench to fully tighten the nuts. To ensure even distribution of stress, tighten the nuts a little at a time, moving from one to another repeatedly in a diagonal pattern. Finally, put the flat, jack, and other tools back into the trunk. Don't bother to replace the hubcap until you get home, but when you do, make sure that the tire valve is correctly positioned, protruding through the hole in the hubcap. You may need to tap the hubcap into place with a rubber mallet.

If correct procedure is followed, most people are able to change a flat tire successfully. Knowing the procedure is no help, however, unless all the necessary tools are in your trunk, along with a properly-inflated spare tire. For this reason, it's important to check the air pressure of the spare from time to time, thereby enabling yourself to use it if necessary.

Cause and Effect

Sometimes called "causal analysis," cause and effect writing attempts to explore the relationship between events and their origins. It can focus on the reasons (causes) for a particular outcome, on the end results themselves (effects), or on both. This can get complicated: one cause can have multiple effects and vice-versa; multiple causes can produce multiple effects; and sometimes a chain of causation exists, in which a cause leads to an effect that becomes the cause of another effect, and so on. In college writing classes, however, the most common kind of assignment involves identifying the several main causes of one effect or the several main effects of one cause. Therefore, this chapter focuses mainly on those approaches.

Like most writing, causal analysis is essentially informative. But it can also be an effective strategy for arguing a point, either by explaining how one or more causes bring about one or more (desirable or undesirable) effects, or by focusing on one or more effects resulting from one or more causes. In other words, the "cause" focus answers the question "Why?" and the "effect" focus answers the question "What?" In this regard, it's useful to understand that causal analysis can be approached in the context of past, present, or future, as in these examples:

Cause	Effect
Why **did** X happen?	What **was** the effect of X?
Why **does** X happen?	What **is** the effect of X?
Why **will** X happen?	What **will be** the effect of X?

In other words, causal analysis can be used to explain events occurring in the past, the present, and the future. Clearly, then, it has broad applications.

POINT OF VIEW

Like most kinds of writing, cause and effect essays ordinarily employ third-person point of view. As already mentioned, there's usually nothing to be gained by using the subjective first-person approach when presenting factual information. The one exception to this would be an essay in which cause and effect were used to discuss the writer's personal experiences in support of the thesis. An example might be an essay in which the writer outlines the negative consequences of substance abuse and draws upon personal experience to illustrate those outcomes. Of course, most essays of any kind seek to argue a point and provide support for the writer's personal opinions, as in the model essay at the end of this section. Nevertheless, unless the examples are of a personal nature, as in the substance abuse essay, a third-person approach is still the better choice because it creates the impression of objectivity and is therefore more persuasive.

ORGANIZATION AND DEVELOPMENT

Like any essay, a cause and effect paper must have a clear thesis statement that establishes the approach to the topic, like this: "Although some overweight people blame their condition on heredity, it seems more likely that our nationwide obesity epidemic is actually the result of two main causes: poor eating habits and lack of exercise."

Notice, however, that this thesis statement carefully avoids overstating its case. The wordings "some people" and "seems more likely" are wise choices, because causation is extremely complex, quite difficult to prove absolutely. For the sake of credibility, therefore, a somewhat tentative thesis statement is always appropriate in causal analysis.

Once the causes are identified, they must be presented in the most effective order. If the causes occur in chronological sequence, then the essay could be arranged that way. But this is not always the case. When arranging non-chronological causes, it's best to begin with the simplest causes and move on to the more complex ones. And, since the points being made in a cause and effect essay are by their nature interrelated, it's helpful to use transitions—words and expressions like "accordingly," "therefore," "as a result," and "consequently"—a bit more often than usual to help the reader make the connections.

KINDS OF CAUSES

There are three main kinds of causes.

- ► Necessary Cause: Something that must happen in order for a given outcome to occur.
  A PIN number is necessary in order to conduct an ATM transaction.

- ► Sufficient Cause: Something that could cause a given outcome.
  Head injuries often result in death.

- ► Precipitating Cause: The final, "triggering" cause in a series of causes in which the first cause results in an effect that then becomes the cause of the following effect, and so on, until the final effect.
  The driver became distracted while texting, veered into oncoming traffic, over-corrected, lost control of his car, swerved off the road, struck a utility pole, and totaled the vehicle.

In the above example, the precipitating cause could also be called the *main* or *direct* or *immediate* cause, while the driver's earlier errors could be called the *contributing* or *indirect* or *remote* causes. These are all common terms in discussions of cause and effect. When writing a causal analysis essay, however, it's unwise to overload the discussion with remote causes because it will not be possible to include them all in three or four body paragraphs without the essay becoming simply a boring catalog or list, rather than an interesting, in-depth discussion.

CAUSATION VS. COINCIDENCE

When writing a causal analysis essay you must avoid the *post hoc ergo propter hoc* fallacy mentioned in Chapter 7. As explained there, this is a Latin phrase meaning "after this, therefore because of this." But X does not necessarily cause Y simply because X happens first. Although there is a chronological sequence of events, there may or may not be a causal relationship. Consider this example:

> Tyler had a heated argument with his brother this morning. Therefore, he failed his math exam this afternoon.

While it's safe to say that the argument probably didn't *improve* Tyler's powers of concentration (or his knowledge of math), there is no proof that it caused him to flunk the test. The fact that the argument and the exam happened on the same day is mere coincidence. There were probably a great many other, more influential reasons for Tyler's failure. Most of us are able to recognize and avoid the *post hoc* fallacy when considering everyday situations such as Tyler's, but it's a bit more difficult when writing about complex subject matter. So it's important to remember that without valid evidence, there is no justification for assuming causation.

RESEARCH-BASED CAUSAL ANALYSIS

As in any information-based essay, a causal analysis paper's claims must be valid assertions, reinforced by evidence. This often requires research in order to gather proof—statistics, quotes, verifiable facts. Although a causal analysis essay need not become a full-blown research project, there's nothing wrong with using quotation, paraphrase, or other supporting details from reputable sources to bolster your discussion. As always when using outside sources, you must somehow acknowledge those authorities, either by using formal MLA documentation or simply by providing acknowledgement in the body of the paper, as in the sample essay at the end of this chapter, in which a professor's remarks are quoted to support the writer's assertions.

CHECKLIST: CAUSE & EFFECT ESSAY

A good cause and effect-based essay

- ► Has a meaningful title that clearly identifies the topic

- ► Opens with an interesting, attention-getting introduction that again identifies the topic, establishes its significance, and provides a firm thesis statement

- ► Is organized into three or four body paragraphs, covering the topic in a coherent, step-by-step way, focusing on one main idea at a time, in logical sequence

- ► Focuses on *either* causes or effects

- ► Provides enough concrete, specific detail to fully develop the ideas

- ► Avoids the *post hoc ergo hoc* fallacy

- ► Closes with a smooth, satisfying conclusion that gracefully resolves the discussion by somehow relating back to the introduction

- ► Uses clear, simple, straightforward language—nothing fancy

- ► Maintains an appropriate tone, neither too formal nor too conversational

- ► Contains no inappropriate material

- ► Contains no typos or mechanical errors in spelling, capitalization, punctuation, or grammar

- ► Satisfies the length requirements of the assignment

MODEL CAUSE & EFFECT ESSAY

The Keys to Academic Success in College

When you hear that a friend of yours made the college honor roll by earning straight A's last semester, you're probably impressed and maybe a little envious too. But there's really no need for jealousy, because you could probably perform just as well yourself. Academic excellence is within the reach of any student who understands what's required: attending regularly, paying attention and participating in class, studying enough, and completing assignments, tests, and exams satisfactorily.

Obviously, regular attendance is fundamental. Students who are frequently late or absent miss important lecture material and in-class activities. In addition, they are often unaware of assignments and other requirements mentioned by the instructor, and wind up handing in late or incorrect work, thereby receiving low grades. As Professor George Searles of Mohawk Valley Community College explains, "When I compute the final averages at the end of the semester, there's always a direct correlation between attendance and grades. Students who show up at least 90% of the time nearly always do well, while those with an attendance mark of 70% or lower often get a D or an F. To hit the ball, you have to swing the bat. But first you've got to show up at the ballpark."

But it's not enough to simply sit there in class every day. To extend Professor Searles's metaphor, batters who fail to keep their eye on the ball don't get many hits. So paying close attention in class is very, very important. In addition to listening carefully to the instructor's lectures and feedback from classmates, it's necessary to take good notes that will facilitate home study and review. A good rule of thumb is that for every hour spent in class you should spend an hour outside of class revisiting the material.

Equally crucial is the need to be fully aware of the rules governing assignments. If in doubt, ask—either in class or afterwards. Most instructors don't mind providing clarification, especially if an assignment is complex or potentially confusing. And nearly all instructors welcome constructive in-class participation in the form of relevant questions and comments in response to the material. The student who sits up front, conveys a positive, engaged attitude, and expresses interest in the subject matter always does better than someone who retreats to the back of the room, tunes out, and spends the class period texting.

Simple enough, then: Attend regularly, pay attention, and hit the books with willingness and enthusiasm. These are the keys. They'll unlock the door to academic success for you, as they've done for your friend. And once that door is open, you can go right through it to achieve your goal: a college transcript you can be proud of.

EXERCISES

1. Choose one of the following topics and write a well-organized, fully-developed **narrative** essay of 500–750 words.

   ▶ A Very Embarrassing Moment
   ▶ A Very Angry Moment
   ▶ A Very Satisfying Accomplishment
   ▶ My Best Summer
   ▶ What I Expect My Life To Be Like in Ten Years

2. Choose one of the following topics and write a well-organized, fully-developed **definition** essay of 500–750 words.

   ▶ Existentialism
   ▶ Feminism
   ▶ Title IX
   ▶ Socialism
   ▶ Political Correctness

3. Choose one of the following topics and write a well-organized, fully-developed **description** essay of 500–750 words.

   ▶ My Most Interesting Relative
   ▶ My English Professor's Office
   ▶ The Street Where I Live
   ▶ My Favorite Bar/Restaurant/Nightclub
   ▶ My Ideal Boyfriend/Girlfriend (or Husband/Wife)

4. Choose one of the following topics and write a well-organized, fully-developed **exemplification** essay of 500–750 words.

   ▶ Mindless Reality Shows
   ▶ Sexual Harassment in the Workplace
   ▶ Advantages (or Disadvantages) of Dormitory Living
   ▶ Benefits of Participating in Extracurricular Activities
   ▶ Muscle Cars

5. Choose one of the following topics and write a well-organized, fully-developed **comparison/contrast** essay of 500–750 words.

   ▶ Two Generations' Clothing Styles
   ▶ Train Travel vs. Air Travel
   ▶ Basketball vs. Golf
   ▶ City Life vs. Country Life
   ▶ Poetry vs. Fiction

6. Choose one of the following topics and write a well-organized, fully-developed **process analysis** essay of 500–750 words.

    ► How To Prepare a Western Omelet
    ► How To Program a Digital Wristwatch
    ► How To Create a Playlist on an MP3 Player
    ► How To Create a Facebook Page
    ► How To Sell on eBay

7. Choose one of the following topics and write a well-organized, fully-developed **cause and effect** essay of 500–750 words.

    ► The Health Hazards of Cigarette Smoking
    ► The Effects of Online News Sites On Print Media
    ► The Causes of Prejudice Against Immigrants
    ► The Effects of Global Warming
    ► The Causes of Political Apathy

PART 4

Specialized Essays

Regardless of its purpose and its intended audience, and irrespective of which strategy has governed its development, every essay reflects the basic features of the essay genre. Nevertheless, there are certain specialized situations in which the writer of an essay must adapt to atypical circumstances. Foremost among these are assignments requiring the composition of an *essay examination* or a *literary criticism essay*. Both of these situations pose unique challenges, as discussed in the following chapters.

CHAPTER 9

Essay Examinations

LEARNING OBJECTIVES

When you complete this chapter, you will be able to

- ► Recognize key words in an essay exam to understand the question and provide the kind of answer the directions require
- ► Complete take-home exams successfully by performing the three-step process of pre-writing, writing, and rewriting, and providing any necessary documentation
- ► Complete in-class exams successfully by practicing efficient time-management

In practically every college course, regardless of subject area, students are expected to demonstrate their knowledge of the material by completing quizzes and tests. If only short answers are required, the most typical formats are multiple-choice and fill-in-the-blanks. For in-depth responses, however, the essay examination is the norm. In many respects, writing an essay exam is essentially the same as writing any other essay. Your audience, for example, is still your professor. Accordingly, your tone should remain rather formal. But there are some significant differences, particularly if the exam is an in-class assignment rather than a take-home. When you complete this chapter you'll be ready to successfully complete both kinds of essay exams.

UNDERSTANDING THE QUESTION

Whether you're writing in-class or at home, the single most important factor in writing any essay exam is that you must *answer the question*. A common error is to overlook part of the question or to provide a different kind of answer from what the directions require. To prevent this, you should read the question (and the directions!) several times to ensure that you fully understand them. Be alert for specific commands that signal the type of answer that's expected. Here's a list of ten such terms:

- ► *Analyze*: Break a subject down into its parts to reveal its meaning, nature, or significance.
- ► *Compare/Contrast*: Show similarities and/or differences between two or more things.
- ► *Define*: Provide a clear statement of the literal meaning of a word, expression, or concept.
- ► *Describe*: Use specific details to create a visual image in the mind's eye.
- ► *Discuss*: Talk in a general but meaningful and enlightening way about a specific subject.
- ► *Evaluate*: Make an informed, evidence-supported judgment about the merits (and/or demerits) of something.
- ► *Explain*: Expound on a subject to make it understandable and/or defensible.
- ► *Identify*: Establish the identity or essential nature of something.

▶ *Summarize*: Create a concise restatement of something.

▶ *Trace*: Show the development of a process through its sequential stages.

Each of these verbs requires a different—and very specific—approach, and you must respond accordingly. For example, if you simply summarize when the question asks you to discuss, you shouldn't expect a high grade. Indeed, you might very well fail. On the other hand, if you discuss when the question asks you to summarize, you're guilty of overkill, which most professors find irritating. Try to gear your answer, and the way you frame it, to the approach required by the wording of the question. If you're not sure what's expected, raise your hand and ask. And don't be shy about that. There are probably other students who share your uncertainty and they'll also benefit from any clarification the professor might provide in response to your inquiry.

TAKE-HOME EXAMS

The most basic thing to remember about take-home exams is that they're no different from any other kind of essay. To produce a good exam you must follow the usual three-step procedure: pre-writing, writing, rewriting. And essay exams follow the usual essay format: title, introduction (including a firm thesis statement), body paragraphs, and conclusion. And they are developed using the same approaches explained in Part 3. But *which* approach you use will be determined by the wording of the question.

A key feature of take-home exams is that you can research your topic, drawing upon your textbooks and other resources. But you must be certain you're providing full documentation, using MLA, APA, or whatever other style the professor requires, to avoid committing plagiarism.

IN-CLASS EXAMS

No matter what the question and the required approach, an in-class exam poses certain challenges beyond those of a take-home. For starters, there's a time limit. Obviously, this restricts your ability to pre-write and rewrite. As explained in Part 2, however, writing is a process and those two steps remain crucial. It would be a big mistake to simply plunge into your essay without some planning, or to hand it in without fine-tuning it a bit at the end of the allotted time. But you have to accomplish these steps a lot faster than you would if writing at home. In a one-hour class period, for example, you might allow approximately ten minutes for pre-writing, forty minutes for writing, and ten minutes for rewriting. In a longer class period, you could pre-write and rewrite a little more. But even then you'd have to hurry, holding your pre-writing and rewriting to no more than fifteen minutes each.

As a result, an in-class essay cannot be as polished as a homework assignment, and no reasonable professor expects it to be. Unless the exam is written for an English class, your professor will probably be far more interested in the *content* of your essay than in your spelling, punctuation, and grammar. In other words, your grade will depend mostly on how well and how fully you respond to the question. That's not to say, however, that you can completely ignore the mechanical aspects. Your writing should always be as professional and error-free as you can make it. One very helpful strategy is to firmly memorize the correct spelling of any names or specialized terms relating to what you've studied during the semester. And if any such words actually appear in the question itself, make *absolutely* certain that you get them right. Most professors are reasonably tolerant of the occasional miscue, but careless—and therefore inexcusable—misspellings will probably lower your grade.

At the rewriting step in the process, therefore, you should revise not only for content and organization but also for obvious errors. If handwriting rather than working on a computer, don't be afraid to cross out or erase. You can provide margin notes or arrows indicating the repositioning of words, sentences, or whole paragraphs. Sloppy and strong is better than neat and weak. Make sure, though, that all revisions and changes are easy to read and understand. If the exam is so messy that it's hard to follow, the grade will almost certainly suffer.

Another difference between an in-class essay exam and one written at home is that the introduction of the in-class piece need not be as fully developed. Given the time constraints of the in-class situation, it makes more sense to focus your energies on the body paragraphs because that's really where you must showcase your understanding of the subject matter. Indeed, the introductory paragraph of an in-class essay exam is sometimes little more than a rewording of the question. Here's an example from an introductory psychology course:

> **QUESTION:** In a well-organized, fully-developed essay, explain the differences between neurosis and psychosis, and provide examples of behaviors that might be considered typical of each.

> **INTRODUCTION:** There is a firm distinction between neurosis and psychosis, and certain behaviors that are typical of each condition illustrate the differences between the two.

Similarly, the conclusion of an in-class essay can also be rather brief, as little as two or three sentences summarizing what's been said. The same is true of take-home exams in subjects other than English. The one exception to all this would be an English composition exam designed to test your knowledge of essay structure. In that situation, you'd need a fully developed introduction and conclusion in addition to your several body paragraphs.

CHECKLIST: ESSAY EXAMINATION

A good essay exam

▶ Has a meaningful title that clearly identifies the topic

▶ Opens with an interesting, attention-getting introduction that again identifies the topic and provides a firm thesis statement

▶ *Answers the question* (rather than some other question) by responding appropriately to key verbs in the phrasing of the question

▶ Is organized into three or four body paragraphs, covering the topic in a coherent, step-by-step way, focusing on one main idea at a time, in logical sequence

▶ Provides enough concrete, specific detail to fully develop the ideas

▶ Closes with a smooth, satisfying conclusion that gracefully resolves the discussion by somehow relating back to the introduction

▶ Uses clear, simple, straightforward language—nothing fancy

▶ Maintains an appropriate tone, neither too formal nor too conversational

▶ Contains no inappropriate material

▶ Contains no typos or mechanical errors in spelling, capitalization, punctuation, or grammar

▶ Satisfies the length requirements of the assignment

EXERCISES

Here's an actual midterm essay exam from a first-year English composition course, along with three students' responses. Which of the three is the best essay in response to the exam? Why? What are the shortcomings of the other two?

Midterm Examination

In a well-organized essay, fully describe three visible articles of clothing that you are wearing right now. Your descriptions should be detailed enough so that someone reading your essay could pick you out of the crowd. In addition, explain how, where, and when you got each article and—if you know—how much it cost. Lastly, select one of the three articles and discuss in some depth what you think it suggests about your personality.

ESSAY EXAM #1

My Clothes

What am I wearing today? A baseball hat, a sweatshirt, a short skirt, knee-high socks, and my Uggs shoes. All of these things say alot about who I am.

The baseball hat has the Yankee's logo on the front. What it shows is that I'm a huge Yankees fan. My whole family loves the Yankees. We try to go to at least one game at Yankee Stadium every year. It's very expensive, but it's worth it. Until he retired, Derek Jeter was my favorite player. I still love the team, but the Yankees just aren't the same without him.

My sweatshirt says "Central High Basketball" on the front in red letters, with a picture of a basketball underneath. I got this shirt for free because I was on the team in high school. When I was a senior we had a pretty good year, winning most of our games and going to the regionals. In our last game I scored seventeen points, but we lost. The score was something like 50–35. We never really had a chance because those girls were really, really tall and they had this one girl who seemed to make every shot she tried.

My skirt is made of jeans material and, like I said, its short. But even though its pretty cold today I'm not to uncomfortable because I'm also wearing the knee-high socks and my Uggs, which are really warm and comfortable. I guess that shows that I like to be comfortable.

So that's what I have on today. To be honest, I didn't really think alot about what I was putting on this morning because I overslept and was rushing around, just grabing whatever was laying around. But I think I look pretty good anyway, and that's important to me too.

ESSAY EXAM #2

Three Articles of Clothing

Most people like to look good. I know I do. Part of looking good is figuring out how to dress in a way that suits your body type and personality. When I got dressed for school this morning I was keeping that in mind, just like I do everyday. I think the outfit I came up with today is a good one. Let me tell you about three of the things I'm wearing. My hoodie, my tights and my sneakers.

The hoodie is a slightly oversized pullover (no zipper down the front) and is pure white. It has no writting on it. I prefer not to wear clothes with slogans or anything like that, unless it's a designer logo. Actually this hoodie does have a very small black Nike "swoosh" on the left side of the front. I paid about twenty-five dollars for it on sale. I think it looks very clean and attractive.

My tights are just ordinary ballet-style tights, in black. I think I look good in tights because I'm slim, and the contrast between the baggy white hoodie and the sleek black tights is effective and attention-getting. I bought these tights last month at the Danskin outlet in the South Side mall.

On my feet I'm wearing basketball sneakers made by Converse—the kind that people call "Chucks." The sneakers are low-cut and black. I like the way the black color of the shoes echoes the color of the tights and even the Nike "swoosh" on my hoodie. I actually received these Chuck's as a birthday present from my sister, who knew I'd been wanting a new pair ever since my old ones wore out.

Really everything I'm wearing today reflects my personality. As I said in the introduction, I like to look good, and I think this outfit makes that happen. It's simple yet elegant and eye-catching, and the Chuck's add a little hint of something a little adventureous, which is always good if you want to look interesting.

ESSAY EXAM #3

Three Articles of Clothing I'm Wearing Today

Many countries have specific styles of dress or articles of clothing that are associated with those cultures. Consider hats, for example: The beret is thought of as essentially French, while the derby originated in England, and the sombrero is worn principally in Mexico. In the United States, many styles of clothing can be seen, because of the diversity of our population. In this essay I will describe and discuss three articles of clothing I'm wearing today, and will attempt to explain what one of them reflects about my personality.

At this moment I'm wearing my favorite sweater. It's a long-sleeved, crew neck, navy-blue pullover with an approximately one-inch red stripe that runs horizontally across my chest. It's a size large. My mother gave it to me last Christmas. I don't know where she bought it or how much she paid, but I think it was probably fairly expensive because it has a substantial feel to it and has held up very well for almost a year now, even though I wear it often.

On my feet I'm wearing Asics running shoes, model number GT-2110, size 10. They're basically white, trimmed in gray, navy blue, and reflective silver and gold. On the back of each shoe is a label that reads "GEL," with the letters arranged vertically. Just below, in horizontal letters, is the label "I•G•S." I'm not entirely sure what the labels actually mean, but I once read that "Asics" stands for "animus sanus in corpore sano" (Latin for "a sound mind in a sound body"). I bought these shoes at the Foot Locker store in the Cantortown Mall. They cost about eighty dollars—expensive but worth it, because I run a lot.

Lastly, I'm wearing basic Lee jeans, size 30/32. They have two pockets in the front (with a smaller "watch pocket" sort of inside the right pocket, but still visible just below the waist line) and two square, stitched-on pockets in the back. These jeans have a total of seven belt loops and the rectangular leather Lee logo patch that can also serve as a belt loop on the right in the back. I bought these jeans about two years ago at Bernstein's Army & Navy on Main Street, which has since gone out of business. If I remember correctly, they cost about thirty dollars.

I like all three of these items, but I think the one that says the most about me personally would be the Lee jeans. Practically everybody wears jeans, but mine are different, because they are both traditional and unconventional at the same time, just like me. They're traditional because they're cut normally, not oversized or decorated with zippers and snaps, and they're a fairly well-known brand. But they are not blue or black like most of the jeans you'll see people wearing. Mine are gray, a rather unusual color for jeans. So, as I said, the jeans—like me—are typical but quite atypical all at once.

You're probably wondering what exactly I mean when I claim to be, like my jeans, "traditional and unconventional at the same time...typical but quite atypical all at once." Well, the traditional and typical part is plain to see. For better or worse, nothing about my appearance—except maybe my gray jeans—or usual behavior would cause anyone to notice me. But there's another whole side to me that's not immediately obvious: a highly individualistic, even somewhat eccentric dimension. Want details? Sorry, but that's a subject for another whole essay altogether.

CHAPTER 10

Literary Criticism

LEARNING OBJECTIVES

When you complete this chapter, you will be able to

- ► Write a successful essay of literary criticism that correctly explicates the content of a literary work by applying a specific critical perspective
- ► Write a successful essay of literary criticism that correctly explicates the form of a literary work by applying the principles of formalist criticism
- ► Write a successful essay of literary criticism that incorporates the unique features of essays of literary criticism

Writing about literature is known as *literary criticism*. Ordinarily when we criticize, we're finding fault. In this context, however, criticism simply means interpretation, analysis, discussion—and, ultimately, evaluation. Granted, we may finally decide that the work under consideration is flawed in one way or another. However, the main purpose of literary criticism is not to point out weaknesses but to clarify the meaning of a work and/or the methods by which the author created it. In the college setting, this typically involves writing an essay.

A literary criticism essay is fundamentally no different from any other essay. As already explained, an essay should have a title, an introduction with a firm thesis statement, three or four body paragraphs, and a conclusion. And, as always, if you're quoting from outside sources or incorporating information gathered from research, the essay must also include full documentation. Literary criticism is different from other kinds of essay writing, however, because you must decide upon a *critical perspective* before you can begin.

The task of literary criticism is further complicated by the fact that in a given work, several critical perspectives may overlap. For example, many feminist works that portray discrimination against women are colored by the historical reality that such injustice has been a fundamental feature of many societies throughout recorded time. Accordingly, the Marxist perspective becomes relevant because of women's traditional dependence on men for financial support. Of course, these complexities are at work in so-called "real life" as well as in literature. Indeed, that's why literary criticism has value. To better understand literature is to better understand the human predicament.

CRITICAL PERSPECTIVES

There are a variety of critical perspectives—that is, angles from which to approach a work of literature. As mentioned, there is often some overlap among these perspectives, but each is rather different from the others. Here are some of the most common:

Biographical

In what ways have the author's own background and life experience influenced the work? To what extent is the work autobiographical? In what ways—if any—does our knowledge of the author's life help us interpret the work? Biographical criticism seeks to answer one or more of these questions.

Historical

Every work is written in a certain place at a certain time, and most works are set in a particular place and time. In what ways have the known attitudes and cultural assumptions of locations and eras influenced the author or the characters and events depicted?

Mythological

Sometimes called the *archetypal* approach, and drawing upon the famous psychologist Carl Jung's theory of the "collective unconscious," the mythological approach explores the ways, if any, that the work echoes ideas or themes central to the famous myths of the ancient world, thereby reaffirming timeless, universal truths. The Myth of Sisyphus, the Myth of Icarus, and the Myth of Oedipus come immediately to mind as examples of myths that many later writers have invoked—sampled, if you will—to give shape and meaning to their own works.

Marxist

What is the role of money and materialism in the work? How do those considerations influence the narrative voice and/or the characters? To what extent does the work reinforce or challenge the norms of capitalism as opposed to the contrasting principles of socialism?

Feminist

What is the role of gender in the work? In what ways are the characters and situations influenced, shaped, or limited by society's differing assumptions about and expectations of women and men?

Psychological

Based on the pioneering work of Freud, Jung, and Adler in the early twentieth century, this approach seeks to determine how the characters' inner workings (their subconscious fears, obsessions, compulsions, and the like) explain their behavior and the consequent events of the plot—and, similarly, how the *author* might have been influenced by psychological considerations.

Deconstructionist

In what ways does the work contradict itself, creating justification for interpretations not immediately obvious to the reader—perhaps not even intended by the author? And what does this suggest about the nature of literature in general, about writers' intentions and readers' expectations—indeed, about all interpretation of human experience, whether actual or fictional?

Formalist

The most traditional approach, formalism de-emphasizes biographical, historical, and other considerations and attempts to focus only on the work itself, its structural and aesthetic elements. Because the formalist approach can explore so many different features of a literary work, it warrants separate discussion.

FORMALIST CRITICISM

Here are some of the most common areas of concern in the formalist approach:

Title

Nearly all literary works have titles, which function much like the titles of essays. Their purpose is to orient the reader by somehow forecasting what lies ahead. In literature, however, titles are sometimes ironic, suggesting something directly opposite to what the work finally delivers. In any case, it's a mistake to ignore the titles of literary works; they always function meaningfully.

Narrative Perspective

There are basically two ways to tell a story: "I did this, I did that" or "He did this, he did that." The first is called first-person narration, in which a character in the story tells the story. The second is called authorial (or omniscient) narration, in which the author is not a participant in the action but simply reports it. Each approach has its advantages, and anyone who sits down to compose a fictional narrative must decide which to use. Some writers—the American novelist Jennifer Egan, for example—may use both within a given work.

The first-person approach makes the action seem somehow more "real" and immediate. But a first-person narrator's knowledge of events is necessarily somewhat limited because, just as in actuality, one person cannot know for sure what other people are thinking and usually does not know everything about the situation—background, for example. Hence the first-person narrator may well be an *unreliable* narrator, one whose version of reality cannot be trusted and may in fact lend itself to deconstructive interpretation. As an example, consider the unnamed narrator of Robert Browning's famous (and disturbing) poem "Porphyria's Lover" or, for that matter, Browning's unnamed duke in "My Last Duchess." An authorial narrator, on the other hand, knows all; that's what "omniscient" means—all-knowing. So an omniscient narrator can be trusted to "get it right." Unless the narrative is a memoir, though, it's always a mistake to assume that a first-person narrator is a stand-in for an author writing autobiography or fiction based on autobiography. In fiction, every narrator is an invention created by the author.

Setting

As mentioned in the above discussion of historically-oriented criticism, every actual event occurs in a particular place at a particular time. When an author writes a story, therefore, the fictitious events must be grounded in place and time in order to be convincing. Naturally, the author will try to choose wisely, selecting a setting appropriate to the narrative's purposes. It's no accident, for example, that the fictitious city of

Dempsey in Richard Price's novel *Clockers* (about urban drug dealers) was modeled on the Jersey City slums, which are among the northeast's grittiest.

Conflict

Without conflict—a clash of some sort, X vs. Y—there's no story. By identifying a work's central oppositions we come to a clearer sense of what the story's really all about. As briefly outlined in Chapter 8, there are several basic kinds of conflict:

▶ **Individual vs. Self**: Sometimes called "inner conflict," this always involves a person trying to choose between competing impulses. Usually it's a "good vs. evil" situation, but not always; the character may be trying to decide between the lesser of two evils, or between the greater of two goods. Many of Shakespeare's heroes struggle with such dilemmas.

▶ **Individual vs. Individual**: Essentially the "good guy vs. bad guy" scenario, but the variations are virtually unlimited: child vs. parent, wife vs. husband, worker vs. boss, and so on. In short, one person against another—or, collectively, "us vs. them."

▶ **Individual vs. Society**: The person in conflict with the group, a common theme in much science fiction. Usually the protagonist is an enlightened non-conformist refusing to accept the norms of a repressive or otherwise mistaken community. Often, the individual pays dearly for this oppositional stance, despite its validity. Think Romeo and Juliet, or Winston Smith in George Orwell's novel *1984*.

▶ **Individual vs. Nature**: The person in conflict with the great natural forces: fire, tornado, flood, blizzard, earthquake, and the like. Sometimes, however, nature is represented by the animal kingdom, as in the *Jaws* movies or Alfred Hitchcock's famous film *The Birds*.

▶ **Individual vs. Fate**: Sometimes called "Individual vs. God (or the gods)," this conflict nearly always operates to the individual's disadvantage, as might be expected. By definition, fate has the upper hand. Resistance may be noble but is usually futile. Oedipus, for example, does everything in his power to prevent the fulfillment of prophecy, but to no avail. Indeed, his actions ensure that the awful prophecy *will* be fulfilled.

Irony

Authors are particularly fond of this device, which basically involves reversal of expectation. The word derives from the *eiron*, a stock character in ancient Greek comedy who pretends to be unsophisticated but is actually wise. There are three kinds of irony in literature:

▶ **Verbal Irony**: Related to sarcasm, verbal irony involves deliberately using words or expressions whose meanings are the opposite of what is meant. Often it functions as a kind of "in joke" between writer and reader, as in Kate Chopin's "The Story of an Hour" (like much of Chopin's work, an exceptionally ironic story on many levels), in which the narrator says

> Her husband's friend Richards was there, too, *near her.* It was he who had been in the newspaper office when intelligence of the railroad disaster was received, with Brently Mallard's name leading the list of "killed." He had only taken the time to *assure* himself of its truth by a second telegram, *and had hastened to forestall any less careful, less tender friend in bearing the sad message.*

The wording that's been italicized here is clearly ironic because Richards is obviously attracted to Mrs. Mallard, and may well be experiencing mixed emotions—some of them self-serving—in response to the news that her husband appears to have been killed.

▶ **Dramatic Irony**: Like verbal irony, this involves a discrepancy between actuality and what is said. But the difference is that in this case the speaker is unaware of the discrepancy. Although most common in plays, it functions in fiction and poetry as well. To cite another example from "The Story of an Hour," we learn that the doctors believe Mrs. Mallard's fatal heart attack has been caused by "joy that kills" when actually she has died of heartbreak.

▶ **Situational Irony**: This occurs when the expected or desired outcome of a situation is thwarted or reversed—often with tragic consequences—for no valid reason. For example, Romeo kills himself because he thinks that Juliet is dead when in fact she is not.

Symbolism

This device involves details that the author has deliberately inserted into the work because they operate on more than one level. They are details that may indeed be present in "real life" but have been carefully selected for their particular significance. For example, in Shirley Jackson's famous short story "The Lottery" (in which the winner is killed) Old Man Warner brags that he has participated seventy-seven times. Obviously, Jackson could have used any large number but chose seventy-seven because of its connotations ("lucky sevens"). Colors are often used this way because certain colors connote certain ideas. Red, for example, can symbolize danger or sexuality, while blue is associated with sadness, and yellow can suggest either decay or cowardice. Names can also function symbolically. To cite "The Lottery" once more, the two men who officiate at the deadly event every June are Mr. *Summers* and Mr. *Graves*. And Old Man *Warner*, of course, is a warn-er who counsels the townspeople about the imagined dangers of ending the lottery. Indeed, most of the names in "The Lottery" are symbolic on some level.

UNIQUE FEATURES OF THE LITERARY CRITICISM ESSAY

Everything that's been said so far applies to writing about all three of the principal literary genres: poetry, fiction, and drama. Regardless of genre, any essay of literary criticism exhibits certain features unique to that kind of writing. Here they are:

▶ **Title**: The title of a literary criticism essay should include three things: the name of the work being discussed, the name of the author who wrote it, and a meaningful phrase that clearly indicates the essay's approach. If you're having trouble writing a good title, you probably haven't really decided what you're trying to say. For example, a title like "The Catcher in the Rye" tells the reader what work will be discussed but provides no clue as to where the discussion is headed. In all likelihood, the writer doesn't know, and needs to go back to the pre-writing stage and find out. Here's a much better title, one that clearly indicates what lies ahead and reflects thoughtful planning by the student writer: "Innocence vs. Experience in J.D. Salinger's *The Catcher in the Rye*." Always try for that level of specificity.

▶ **Introduction**: To open an essay of literary criticism, it's customary to begin with a few sentences of generalization about the author, work, or literary technique you'll be discussing. But, as in any essay, those first few sentences should lead logically and smoothly to a firm thesis statement at or very near the end of that opening paragraph. The essay's thesis statement and the title should echo each other. The title is a short version of the thesis statement, while the thesis statement is an expanded version of the title. In our hypothetical *Catcher in the Rye* essay, the thesis statement might be something like this: "This novel includes several key scenes in which pure, child-like innocence comes into conflict with more-worldly behaviors, thereby highlighting some of the book's main themes."

► **Plot Summary:** While *some* plot summary is appropriate in order to create context at the beginning of the essay, you must very quickly move past it and begin a discussion of more-substantial issues. A literary criticism essay must not simply re-tell the story. When you do refer to plot developments, though, be sure to phrase those references in present tense rather than in past tense. Why? Because, unlike events in "real life," the events in a literary work are not actual occurrences. Usually when we write about the past it's appropriate—indeed, necessary—to use past tense verbs, because those events are over and done with. But the fictitious events in a work of literature exist in a kind of eternal present there on the page. Consider: When Carrie burns down her high school gym in the Steven King novel (and movie) named after her, that gym is in flames whether we are reading the novel (or watching the movie) yesterday, today, or tomorrow. So—to repeat—use present tense, not past tense, when referring to plot developments and do not rely on plot summary alone. Go deeper.

► **Identifying Characters:** Most works of literature—fiction and drama especially—involve at least two or more characters whose interactions essentially constitute the story. To ensure that your discussion moves along smoothly and coherently, therefore, it's important that you somehow identify characters the first time you refer to them. A short, descriptive phrase will accomplish this. For example, the writer of the *Catcher in the Rye* essay would not simply say "Holden feels inferior in some ways to Stradlater" if Stradlater had not been mentioned before. Instead, the writer would identify the character, like this: "Holden feels inferior in some ways to Stradlater, his handsome, athletic roommate."

► **Relevance:** Stick to your thesis. Don't go off on unrelated tangents. Of course, asides and relevant parenthetical remarks can be enlightening, but make sure they do not derail the essay's train of thought. Similarly, resist the urge to "preach." Stay away from the "As everyone knows" or "Ever since the dawn of civilization" approach. And avoid "stage directions" such as "Now I shall attempt to show that…." Just say what you have to say, and if your presentation is coherent, it will be self-explanatory. Distracting phrases like "As you can plainly see" and "From the above it is clear that" actually weaken your essay because they serve no real purpose. Let your discussion speak for itself.

► **Conclusion:** As in any essay, you should pull things together at the end. This can be tricky if your essay has discussed more than one work of literature. The conclusion of such an essay must summarize not only what you've said about the last author or work mentioned, but should put into perspective all the works mentioned in the essay by clearly showing how your thesis interrelates among all of them.

The model essay at the end of this chapter uses the biographical approach to satisfactorily fulfill the requirements of literary criticism.

CHECKLIST: LITERARY CRITICISM ESSAY

A good literary criticism essay

▶ Has a meaningful title that names both the author(s) and works(s) under consideration and clearly indicates the slant of the discussion

▶ Opens with a clear, focused introduction that again names the author(s) and work(s) under consideration and plainly states the thesis

▶ *Says something*, rather than rambling aimlessly or relying on mere plot summary

▶ Is organized into three or four body paragraphs, covering the topic in a coherent, step-by-step way, focusing on one main idea at a time, in logical sequence

▶ Uses present tense for references to plot developments, and briefly identifies characters the first time they're mentioned

▶ Provides enough concrete, specific detail to fully develop the ideas; quotes and other supporting evidence from the literary work itself and/or secondary sources are properly incorporated into the essay

▶ Closes with a smooth, satisfying conclusion that gracefully resolves the discussion by somehow relating back to the introduction

▶ Uses clear, simple, straightforward language—nothing fancy

▶ Maintains an appropriate tone, neither too formal nor too conversational

▶ Contains no inappropriate material

▶ Contains no typos or mechanical errors in spelling, capitalization, punctuation, or grammar

▶ Satisfies the length requirements of the assignment

MODEL LITERARY CRITICISM ESSAY

Autobiographical Elements in Kate Chopin's "The Story of an Hour"

Speaking about the protagonist of his great novel *Madame Bovary*, the French writer Gustave Flaubert once said, "c'est moi" ("this person is me"). Kate Chopin, the American author who penned "The Story of an Hour," might well have said the same about her own protagonist, Louise Mallard. Although there are major differences between the fictional character and Chopin herself, there are many similarities as well—enough, in fact, for us to safely conclude that Chopin based Louise's situation at least partly upon events in her own life.

The plot is simple, though ironic. Louise learns that her husband, Brently, has been killed in a train accident. Rather than becoming upset, she experiences feelings of relief and joy, for she thinks she has been freed from the constraints of marriage. A few minutes later, though, her husband reappears, unharmed. Louise drops dead from shock—and, we can assume, from disappointment as well. Interestingly, Kate Chopin's father had been killed in a railway mishap when she was five years old and her own husband, Oscar, had died in 1882, twelve years before this story was published; like her mother, she never remarried (Toth, "What" 13). We cannot know whether Chopin's feelings toward her own marriage were similar to Louise's, but it's a safe bet that they were not totally dissimilar. The narrator, after all, speaks at one point of Louise's husband's "powerful will bending her in that blind persistence with which men and women believe they have the right to impose a private will upon a fellow-creature." (Chopin 158)

As we know, authors are at liberty to name their characters whatever they choose. It's probably not mere coincidence, then, that Mrs. Mallard is named "Louise," for Chopin was originally from St. Louis, before marrying and relocating to Louisiana. Although the French name "Mallard" is not unknown in the south, it's a slightly uncommon one, and seems like an odd choice, unless we consider that the mallard duck is one of the few species that mate for life. So the name "Louise Mallard" was most likely based on Chopin's personal geography, and also, perhaps, on her feelings about the lifelong nature of wedlock. Often in her work, female characters rebel against the traditional role of wife and mother, as in stories such as "The Storm" and "The Silk Stockings." Her novel *The Awakening* is yet another example; "its sympathetic treatment of adultery shocked reviewers and readers throughout America." (Charters 114)

Finally, there is Brently's friend, Richards. He appears only briefly, once at the beginning of the story and again at the end. It is quite clear that he is attracted to Louise, as evidenced by the fact that he is "near her" when she is told of Brently's supposed death, and by the fact that when Brently walks through the front door, Richards attempts to "screen him from the view of his wife. But...was too late" (Chopin 157, 158). It is as if Richards is almost celebrating Brently's demise, and then trying to deny his resurrection. While there is no hard evidence for such a suggestion, it is at least a possibility that Richards is based on Albert Sampité, with whom the widow is known to have had a scandalous relationship after her husband's death. (Toth, "My" 28)

Of course, there are also major differences between the details of Kate Chopin's life and those of Louise's. For one thing, Oscar Chopin actually died and Brently Mallard does not. And Chopin lived to be 54 years old, while Louise dies as a much younger woman. Further, Chopin was left with six children when her husband died, and there is no mention of children in the story (Toth, "What" 13). Therefore, while Louise is able to imagine that she is "free, free, free" and that "there would be no one to live for . . . she would live for herself" (Chopin 157, 158), the author had no such luxury. And finally, Louise has no apparent role to assume in widowhood, whereas Chopin used her newly single status to pursue her vocation as a writer, giving us an impressive body of work. Her output includes novels, essays, translations, poems, and more than a hundred stories, of which "The Story of an Hour," clearly influenced by her own experiences, is among the best-known. (Charters 114)

Works Cited

Charters, Ann and Samuel Charters. *Literature and Its Writers: A Compact Introduction to Fiction, Poetry, and Drama*. 4th ed., Bedford/St. Martin's, 2007.

Chopin, Kate. "The Story of an Hour." *The Longman Masters of Short Fiction*. Edited by Dana Gioia and R.S. Gwynn. Longman, 2002, pp. 157–58.

Toth, Emily. "My Part in Reviving Kate Chopin." *Awakenings: The Story of the Kate Chopin Reviva*. Edited by Bernard Koloski. Louisiana State UP, 2009, pp. 15–31.

---. "What we do and don't know about Kate Chopin's life." *The Cambridge Companion to Kate Chopin*. Edited by Janet Beer. Cambridge UP, 2008, pp. 13–26.

EXERCISES

Here are two essays of literary criticism dealing with Shirley Jackson's famous short story "The Lottery." Which essay is better? Why? What is the main weakness of the less successful essay?

LITERARY CRITICISM ESSAY # 1

The Lottery

The Lottery is a famous short story about a small town where once a year the people have a lottery. Usually when you think of a lottery you think of it as a good thing, a chance for someone to win something. But this lottery is different. The winner actually *loses* something—their life. Each man in the village must draw a piece of folded paper from the black box. Then after everyone has drawn, the papers are opened and they discover who has the paper with the black dot. At that point everyone in the man's family—the wife, the children, and the man himself—all have to draw again. Whoever gets the black dot this time is immediately stoned to death by everyone else in the village.

In the story Tessie Hutchinson is almost late for the lottery. As she says, she "clean forgot what day it was." But when she remembers, she comes running to the town square, so she's just in time. Mr. Summers and Mr. Graves are the two men in charge of the lottery. Mr. Summers runs the coal company and Mr. Graves is the town's postmaster. Mr. Summers is the one who actually calls out the family names in alphabetical order, so the men can come forward to take their turn.

Some of the people seem to be a little nervous about the lottery. For example, Mrs. Adams says, "some places have already quit lotteries." And Mrs. Delacroix says uneasily, "seems like there's no time at all between lotteries any more . . . . Seems like we got through with the last one only last week." Young Jack Watson has to be told, "Don't be nervous, Jack. Take your time, Son," when it's his turn to draw for his family. (Actually it's just he and his mother, as his father is apparently dead.) Other people, however, seem very supportive of the event. Old Man Warner, who has been in the lottery seventy-seven times, is the most enthusiastic of all. "There's always been a lottery," he points out, after reminding everyone that there "Used to be a saying about 'Lottery in June, corn be heavy soon.'" And Tessie Hutchinson herself seems fully supportive, even urging her husband forward when he hesitates after the Hutchinson family name is called. "Get up there, Bill," she tells him.

After everyone has drawn, it is revealed that Bill Hutchinson has the piece of paper with the black dot on it. Suddenly Tessie has a whole new outlook. "You didn't give him time enough to take any paper he wanted. I saw you. It wasn't fair," she complains. "I think we ought to start over." But nobody listens. The Hutchinsons—Bill, Tessie, and their three children—now all have to pick papers from the box. Whoever gets the black dot this time will be stoned to death by the other people. One by one they open their papers, everyone but Tessie. Bill and the three children each have blank papers, and it becomes obvious that Tessie must be the "winner." Bill must force the paper out of her hand and hold it up so everyone can see the black dot. Then Mr. Summers says, "All right, folks. Let's finish quickly," and Tessie is stoned to death. Her two best friends, Mrs. Delacroix and Mrs. Dunbar, seem especially eager to participate.

Mrs. Delacroix selected a stone so large she had to pick it up with both hands and turned to Mrs. Dunbar. "Come on," she said, "Hurry up." Mrs. Dunbar had small stones in both hands and she said, gasping for breath, "I can't run at all. You'll have to go ahead and I'll catch up with you."

Somebody even gives Tessie's young son Davy some pebbles so that even he can participate in the stoning. That was really sick!

In fact, the whole story is sick. This could never happen in real life. The F.B.I. or some other law enforcement agency would find out about the lottery and put a stop to it. Probably the organizers would be arrested and put in jail where they belong. I know that if I lived in that town, I would move away and not have to participate in this crazy, pointless ritual. I think The Lottery is one of the worst stories I have ever read.

LITERARY CRITICISM ESSAY #2

Symbolism in Shirley Jackson's "The Lottery"

Many writers of serious literature use symbols to help convey the meaning(s) of their work. A symbol is any detail that would perhaps occur in "real life" but which has been carefully selected by the author to achieve maximum significance. Colors, for example, can be symbolic: red traditionally symbolizes danger, yellow is sometimes associated with cowardliness, and green can stand for a variety of things, such as envy, hope, and inexperience. But any detail—not just color—can function symbolically. Shirley Jackson's short story "The Lottery," in which the "winner" is stoned to death, employs various kinds of symbolic details that help to propel the plot and reinforce the author's underlying messages.

Let's begin with numbers. This lottery is traditionally held on June 27, just a few days after the summer solstice (the longest day of the year). In some ancient cultures, many of which worshipped the sun, the summer solstice was a common time for human sacrifice. The belief was that such sacrifices would please the sun, thereby ensuring a good harvest. This connection is reinforced by Old Man Warner, who reminds his fellow villagers, "Used to be a saying about, 'Lottery in June, corn be heavy soon.'" And Warner's age, 77, is also highly significant. The author could just as easily have created a character who was 76 or 78 or any other advanced age, but 77 ("lucky sevens") reinforces the idea that he has repeatedly survived the lottery simply by chance or good luck.

Consider also that the two men who actually conduct the lottery both work at highly appropriate occupations. Mr. Summers operates a coal company. Coal is, of course, black—the color most often associated with death and mourning. Similarly, it's probably no coincidence that the black box resembles a coffin and that at one point it has been stored "underfoot" in the office of Mr. Graves. In his role as the town postmaster, he is responsible for delivering the mail. But in the context of the lottery, he helps to deliver a very specific message: notification of death. Obviously, Shirley Jackson could have provided these two men with any number of occupations, but she selected jobs that would create the appropriate symbolic associations in the reader's subconscious mind.

Significant too is the exchange between Mr. Summers and Tessie Hutchinson near the beginning of the story, when Tessie is nearly late for the gathering. "Thought we were going to have to get on without you, Tessie," Mr. Summers says; she replies, "wouldn't have me leave m'dishes in the sink, now, would you, Joe?" In light of the story's ending, in which Tessie "wins" the lottery and is stoned to death, these comments take on an obviously symbolic—and highly ironic—significance. In a comparable way, Old Man Warner's complaint that "It's not the way it used to be. People ain't the way they used to be" has symbolic meanings that are ironically opposite to what he intends. The whole point of the story is that everything *is* the way it used to be. The lottery does in fact continue, and the people remain generally unopposed to it. Apparently nobody ever really objects to it unless they—as in Tessie's case—are chosen as the "winner." That's the whole problem.

The most obvious symbols in the story are the characters' names. Not all the names function this way, but many—Summers, Graves, Warner, Hutchinson, and others—clearly do. As already mentioned, Mr. Summers and Mr. Graves conduct the annual lottery; as a result of this ritual, every summer there is another grave. Certainly this parallelism must be a deliberate one on the author's part. Likewise, *Old Man Warner* is the symbolic embodiment of tradition, the village's living link to the past; but he is also a warn-er, one who sternly lectures his neighbors about the presumed dangers of abandoning the old ways. It has been suggested that the name Hutchinson is intended to evoke images of the hutch, in which rabbits live. The idea is that this family is representative of the village in general, where people—like scared rabbits—huddle together in their mindless fear, and are therefore always at risk. The names of several minor characters also function in this symbolic way.

In conclusion, Shirley Jackson's "The Lottery" is an excellent and well-known example of how an author can invest a work of fiction with meaningful symbols that create an additional level of resonance. The main message of the story is that our traditions and beliefs are not necessarily correct, and need to be continuously questioned and perhaps revised. Jackson's skillful manipulation of significant details—dates, ages, occupations, comments, names, and other specifics—reinforces the events of the plot, providing a further literary dimension that helps to convey the story's meaning in a highly effective way.

PART 5

Workplace Writing

Nearly all first-year English courses focus mainly on the traditional 500–750 word essay (including essay exams and literary criticism essays). As mentioned in the introduction, however, various other kinds of writing are often covered as well, and that trend is increasing. Accordingly, the chapters in this section explore several types of workplace writing that may be assigned: e-mail, business letters, short reports, proposals, and employment application materials.

CHAPTER 11

E-Mail

LEARNING OBJECTIVES

When you complete this chapter, you will be able to

- ▶ Compose brief but purposeful e-mail messages
- ▶ Achieve the appropriate tone for your audience
- ▶ Observe the principles of e-mail etiquette and avoid common e-mail blunders

By far the most common form of written communication in today's workplace is e-mail, and by now almost everyone is familiar with how to use it. Typically, you log onto the system by typing your name and a secure password that prevents unauthorized access. You can then read any new e-mail listed in the inbox. Depending on your preferences, those messages can be deleted, saved for future reference, printed, answered, or forwarded—or some combination of these options. To respond to a message, you choose the appropriate prompt and insert the reply. To create an entirely new e-mail, choose the appropriate prompt, causing a blank template to appear on the screen, ready to be completed. When you finish the message it can then be sent to as many other persons as you wish simply by typing their e-mail addresses into the TO line. Like replies, this new e-mail is also stored in your electronic SENT file and kept there for future reference.

Virtually all e-mail includes the following features in addition to the message itself:

- ▶ **DATE line**: This is provided automatically and usually includes the *time* of transmission as well.
- ▶ **TO line**: This enables the e-mail to be addressed.
- ▶ **FROM line**: Like the date line, this is provided automatically as soon as the writer logs into the system.
- ▶ **SUBJECT line**: This identifies the topic. Like the title of an essay or the headline on a newspaper story, but even more concisely, the subject line prepares the reader for what's ahead. A good subject line answers this question: "In no more than three words, what is this e-mail about?"

PURPOSE

Although e-mail's usual purpose is to inform, often its secondary purpose is to create an electronic "paper trail"—a written record of a request or other message previously conveyed in person, by phone, or through the grapevine. Accordingly, e-mail comes directly to the point, focusing sharply on what the reader needs to know. Depending on the subject, an e-mail can usually do that in three or four short paragraphs: a concise introduction, a body paragraph or two conveying the details, and perhaps a brief conclusion. But some e-mails are as short as one paragraph or even one sentence. As in all writing, length is determined by purpose and audience.

TONE

The sample e-mail that follows embodies all of the features listed above and provides an opportunity to consider further the principle of *tone* introduced in Chapter 3.

Date: May 7, 2018   9:00 A.M.

To: All Employees

From: Frank Scott

Subject: Ernest Fitzgerald

As you may already know, Ernest Fitzgerald of the Claims Department was admitted to Duval Memorial Hospital over the weekend and is scheduled for surgery tomorrow.

Although Ernie will not be receiving visitors or phone calls for a while, you may want to send him a "Get Well" card to cheer him up. He's in Room 9.

We'll keep you posted on Ernie's progress.

Frank Scott, Director
Human Resources

The personnel director has picked his words carefully to avoid sounding bossy. He says, "You *may want to* send him a get-well card" rather than "You *should*" even though that's what he really means. As this message demonstrates, a tactful writer can soften a recommendation, a request, or even a demand by phrasing it diplomatically.

In the college setting, sometimes students find it necessary to e-mail their professors. They may be seeking clarification of an assignment, explaining an absence, or attending to some other matter. And in the context of online study, such correspondence is of course routine. In any case, however, nearly all professors expect students to observe the norms of conventional spelling, punctuation, and grammar, and to maintain an appropriately respectful tone. Indeed, an overly conversational approach when writing to your professor violates the principles of upward communication explained in Chapter 3 and can cause resentment. If your e-mail opens with a salutation like "Hey, Sarah" (or even "Hey, Prof") it's definitely headed in the wrong direction.

E-MAIL ETIQUETTE

There are good reasons why e-mail has been so universally adopted since becoming available in the 1980s. On the most obvious level, it's incomparably faster than traditional correspondence. In the past, communicating by memo or letter involved at least five distinct steps:

1. Writing
2. Typing (usually by a secretary)
3. Proofreading and initialing by the writer
4. Photocopying for the writer's file
5. Routing to the intended reader(s)

Depending on office workload and clerical staffing levels, this process could become quite time-consuming. With e-mail, however, all five steps are compressed into one, permitting far speedier communication.

Unfortunately, however, the very ease with which e-mail can be produced also creates some problems. In the past, a writer would not bother to write a memo or letter without good reason. Too much time and effort were involved to do otherwise. But now, much needless correspondence is generated. Yesterday's writers would wait until complete information on a given topic had been received, organized, and considered before acting on it or passing it along. But today it's not uncommon for several e-mails to be written on the same subject, doling out the information little by little, sometimes within a very short time-span. The resulting fragmentation wastes the energies of writer and reader alike and increases the possibility of confusion, often because of premature response. One way to minimize this danger is to inspect your entire menu of incoming messages, taking note of multiple messages from the same source or bearing the same subject line, before responding to any.

Similarly, e-mail about sensitive issues is often dashed off "in the heat of battle" without sufficient reflection. In the past, writers could choose to revise or discard a memo if, upon proofreading, it had come to seem a bit too harsh or otherwise inappropriate. But the built-in speed of e-mail eliminates any such opportunity for second thoughts. This can result in counter-productive venting if emotions are not kept under control. Do not hit "Send" until you've had time to cool down and reconsider.

Hasty composition also causes a great many keyboarding miscues, omissions, and other fundamental blunders. These must then be corrected in subsequent messages, creating an annoying flood of "e-mail about e-mail." Indeed, the absence of a secretarial filter has given rise to a great deal of embarrassingly bad writing in the workplace. You risk ridicule and loss of credibility unless you closely proofread every e-mail before sending it. Make sure the information is necessary, accurate, and complete. Fix typos, misspellings, faulty capitalization, sloppy punctuation, and basic grammatical errors. While this is always important, it's especially so when corresponding with readers outside your own workplace. Because you and your outside readers are usually not personally acquainted, a higher level of courteous formality is necessary. Additionally, subject matter is often more involved than that of in-house correspondence, so e-mail sent outside is commonly longer and more fully developed than messages for co-workers. Accordingly, outside e-mail nearly always includes a letter-style salutation and complimentary close.

Here are some additional points to consider about e-mail:

▶ Resist the temptation to forward chain letters, silly jokes, political rants, tasteless images, and the like. This not only wastes people's time but can get you into trouble.

▶ Never forward legitimate e-mails to other readers without the original writer's permission. The message may have been intended for you alone.

▶ Create new e-mail only when necessary, sending only to the person(s) needing it; resist the urge to mass-mail. Similarly, when responding to a mass-mailing do not "Reply All" unless there's a valid reason to do so. Reply only to the sender.

▶ When engaged in a lengthy back and forth exchange, the situation under discussion will evolve. Keep revising your subject line to reflect that.

▶ Because e-mail is only partially able to convey "tone of voice," avoid it in delicate situations—the denial of a request, for example. Instead, use voice mail or actual conversation.

CHECKLIST: E-MAIL

A good e-mail

- ▶ Includes certain features:

    DATE line (date and time appear automatically)

    TO line, which provides the name(s) of the intended reader(s)

    FROM line (writer's name appears automatically)

    SUBJECT line, which is a clear, accurate, but brief statement of what the e-mail is about; usually a word or short phrase is enough

- ▶ Is organized into paragraphs (one is often enough) covering the subject fully in an orderly way

- ▶ Contains no inappropriate material

- ▶ Uses clear, simple, straightforward language—nothing fancy

- ▶ Maintains an appropriate tone, neither too formal nor too conversational

- ▶ Contains no typos or mechanical errors in spelling, punctuation, or grammar

EXERCISES

1. You're the manager of the bookstore at County Community College. The semester is drawing to a close and, as always, students will soon be selling back their textbooks. But the store has decided not to buy back any books on the subject of hospitality management, because that program will be discontinued after the current majors graduate this spring. Students are aware that the program is being terminated, but you must send e-mail notification about the textbook situation.

2. Pressing personal business prevented you from attending your English class yesterday. Send your professor an e-mail apologizing for your absence and requesting to make up any missed work or assignments.

3. The management of the company at which you work has decided to create an employee newsletter that will feature articles about the company, along with general news about trends in the national market. In addition, there will be coverage of employees' personal news—births, marriages, and other noteworthy events and achievements. You have been appointed editor, and your supervisor has asked you to write an e-mail requesting your co-workers to submit any such information they would like included.

4. You are the President of the Liberal Arts Club at your college. With support and oversight from the administration, the club has decided to launch *Literama*, a literary magazine that will feature poetry, fiction, and creative non-fiction. The deadline for submissions—which must be in Microsoft Word—is six weeks from now. Send an e-mail to the student body, asking for submissions. Be sure to provide guidelines about length restrictions and anything else you consider important to mention, including a gently diplomatic explanation that acceptance for publication is not guaranteed.

5. You're the assistant to the Director of Human Resources at a medium-sized company. The crossing gate that prevents unauthorized entry to the employee parking lot can be raised only if the motorist inserts an encoded plastic card into a slot in the control box alongside the gate. Now the system is scheduled for an upgrade. A new box will be installed during this coming weekend, so everyone is required to obtain a new card from the Human Resources Office as soon as possible. To smooth the transition, the gate will be left open until next Wednesday, but after that every employee will need a new card to gain access. Write an e-mail alerting all employees to the situation.

CHAPTER 12

Business Letters

LEARNING OBJECTIVES

When you complete this chapter, you will be able to

- ► Write effective business letters in "full block" format
- ► Write business letters using orderly, three-part organization
- ► Achieve the appropriate tone for your audience

Unlike e-mail, which is used for both internal and external communication, business letters are almost always used for the latter. The business letter conveys a message from someone at Company X to someone elsewhere. And although e-mail is now being used in many situations that formerly required letters, the letter is still preferred for more formal exchanges, especially those in which speed of delivery is not a major factor. And for contacting individual customers and clients (some of whom may still rely on conventional mail), the business letter is obviously the better choice. At least for the immediate future, therefore, the letter will remain a relevant form of workplace correspondence, although its role will almost certainly undergo further redefinition as various forms of electronic communication become increasingly dominant. Ten of the more typical purposes of a letter are as follows:

- ► Sell a product or service (sales)
- ► Request payment (collection)
- ► Purchase a product or service (order)
- ► Voice a complaint (claim)
- ► Respond to a complaint (adjustment)
- ► Ask for information (inquiry)
- ► Provide information (reply)
- ► Thank someone (acknowledgement)
- ► Apply for a job (application)
- ► Recommend someone (reference)

FULL BLOCK FORMAT

Regardless of a letter's purpose, the preferred format today is the *full block* style, in which every line begins at the left margin. These two letters—a consumer claim letter and the adjustment letter in response—both illustrate this layout.

123 Duncan Avenue
Wailsburg, AZ 85000
November 10, 2017

Consumer Relations Department
Top Chef Foods, Inc.
666 Vidrio Street
Albuquerque, NM 87100

Dear Superior Foods:

Top Chef microwave dinners are excellent products that I have purchased regularly for several years. Recently, however, I had an unsettling experience with one of these meals.

While enjoying a liver and lima beans dinner, I discovered in the food what appears to be a thick splinter of glass. I'm sure this is an isolated incident, but I thought your quality control department would want to know about it.

I've enclosed the splinter, taped to the product wrapper, along with the sales receipt for the dinner. May I please be reimbursed $9.98 for the cost?

Sincerely,

G.M. Logan

George M. Logan

Enclosures

Top Chef Foods, Inc.

666 Vidrio Street, Albuquerque, NM 87100   *   (505) 277-1234

November 21, 2017

Mr. George M. Logan
123 Duncan Avenue
Wailsburg, AZ 85000

Dear Mr. Logan:

Thank you for purchasing our product and for taking the time to contact us about it. We apologize for the unsatisfactory condition of your Top Chef microwave dinner.

Quality is of paramount importance to all of us here at Top Chef Foods, and great care is taken in the preparation and packaging of all our products. Our quality assurance staff has been notified of the problem you reported. Although Top Chef Foods does not issue cash refunds, we have enclosed three coupons redeemable at your grocery store for complimentary Top Chef microwave dinners of your choice.

We appreciate this opportunity to be of service, and we hope you will continue to enjoy our products.

Sincerely,

Bernadette Mazur

Bernadette Mazur
Customer Services Department

Enclosures (3)

Notice that full block format employs several required features:

- Single spacing throughout (except between the "blocks" of print, where double-spacing is used)
- Margins of 1 to 1½ inches
- Writer's full address or company letterhead, at the top of the page, followed by the date
- Inside address (reader's full name and address)
- Salutation, followed by a colon (Avoid gender-biased salutations such as "Dear Sir" or "Gentlemen.")
- Complimentary close ("Sincerely" is best), followed by a comma
- Writer's signature
- Writer's full name and title
- Enclosure line (if necessary) to indicate items accompanying the letter

THREE-PART ORGANIZATION

Along with these standard features, all business letters—irrespective of purpose—embrace the same three-part pattern of organization:

1. Brief introductory paragraph establishing context (by referring to previous correspondence, perhaps, or by orienting the reader in some other way) and concisely stating the letter's purpose

2. Body paragraphs (as many as needed) fully conveying the message by providing all necessary details, presented in logical sequence

3. Brief concluding paragraph politely requesting action, thanking the reader, or mentioning any additional facts pertinent to the situation

APPROPRIATE TONE

Like all successful communication, a good letter must adopt an appropriate tone. A letter is more formal than an in-house e-mail because it's more public. Accordingly, a letter should uphold the image of the writer's company or organization by reflecting a high degree of professionalism. But although a letter's style should be polished, the language should be natural and easy to understand. The key to achieving a readable style—in a letter or in anything else you write—is to understand that you should not sound pompous or "official." As mentioned in Chapter 6, writing should sound much like ordinary speech, but polished up. Strive for direct, conversational phrasing. Whatever you do, stay away from stilted, old-fashioned business clichés. Here's a list of overly bureaucratic expressions, paired with "plain English" alternatives:

Cliché	Alternative
As per your request	As you requested
Attached please find	Here is
At this point in time	Now
In lieu of	Instead of
In the event that	If
Please be advised that X	X
Pursuant to our agreement	As we agreed
Until such time as	Until
We are in receipt of	We have received
We regret to advise you that X	Regrettably, X

CHECKLIST: BUSINESS LETTER

A good business letter

- ▶ Follows full block format

- ▶ Includes certain features:

    Writer's complete address (but not the writer's name, which appears only at the bottom of the letter)

    Date

    Reader's full name and complete address (use abbreviations)

    Salutation, followed by a colon

    Complimentary close ("Sincerely" is best), followed by a comma

    Writer's signature and full name

    Enclosure notation, if necessary

- ▶ Is organized into paragraphs, covering the subject fully in an orderly way

    Introductory paragraph establishes context and states the purpose

    Body paragraphs provide all necessary details in logical sequence

    Concluding paragraph politely achieves closure

- ▶ Uses clear, simple, straightforward language—nothing fancy

- ▶ Maintains an appropriate tone, neither too formal nor too conversational

- ▶ Contains no typos or mechanical errors in spelling, punctuation, or grammar

EXERCISES

1. A product that you especially like is suddenly no longer available in retail stores in your area. Write the manufacturer an inquiry letter requesting information about how to place an order for the product.

2. Proceeding as if you've received the information requested in Exercise 1, write a letter ordering the product.

3. Pretend you've received the product ordered in Exercise 2, but it's somehow unsatisfactory. Write the manufacturer a claim letter expressing dissatisfaction and requesting an exchange or refund.

4. Team up with a classmate, exchange the claim letters you each wrote in response to Exercise 3, and then write adjustment letters to each other.

5. Write an acknowledgment letter to the editor of either your campus newspaper or a regional daily, expressing your approval of some meaningful contribution made by a local person or organization.

CHAPTER 13

Short Reports

LEARNING OBJECTIVES

When you complete this chapter, you will be able to

- ► Use basic principles of page design to create short reports that are visually appealing
- ► Write short reports of several different kinds: incident reports, progress reports, recommendation reports, travel reports, and lab reports

Like e-mail and letters, reports are an important form of on-the-job communication, and are often assigned in college courses as well. They can be internal or external documents and they follow certain standard conventions. In several respects, however, reports are quite different from e-mail and letters. For example, a report is rarely just a written account of information the reader already knows. Nearly always, the report's subject matter is new information. The reader may be acquainted with the general outlines of the situation the report explores but not with the details. Quite often, in fact, the reader will have requested the report just to get those details. And in the college setting, of course, the report's purpose is to demonstrate the results of an experiment or some other assigned exercise. In any case, reports communicate information that's too complicated for an e-mail or letter. Simply stated, there are two kinds of reports: short and long. This chapter focuses on the former.

PAGE DESIGN

As we have seen, the physical appearance of e-mail and letters is determined by established guidelines that vary only slightly. But reports, though also subject to certain conventions, are to a far greater extent the creation of individual writers who determine not only their content but also their physical appearance. This is significant because our ability to comprehend what we read is greatly influenced by how it looks on the page or screen. Therefore, a report should not appear difficult or intimidating. Instead, it should be visually appealing. This can be achieved by observing some basic design principles. Here they are:

- ► **Legible Type:** Although many different typefaces and type sizes exist, most readers respond best to 12-point type using both uppercase and lowercase letters, like this text. Anything smaller or larger is difficult to read, as is the all-capitals approach. Such variations are useful only in major headings or to emphasize a particular word or phrase.
- ► **Generous Margins:** Text should be framed by ample white space. Top and bottom margins should be at least 1 inch and side margins 1¼ inches. If the report is to be printed out and stapled or bound, the left-hand margins should be 2 inches. (If the report is to be duplicated back-to-back before stapling or binding, the 2-inch margin should be on the *right* side of the even-numbered pages.) The right

margin should not be justified, but should be left ragged. This improves legibility by creating length variation from line to line.

► **Textual Divisions:** To organize a report's content, related paragraphs should be grouped together into separate sections, sequenced in a manner that logically reflects the nature of the information. Like those in an academic essay, paragraphs in a report should not exceed five or six sentences (unless some of the sentences are very short) and should be separated by ample white space. If the paragraphs are single spaced, insert double spacing between them. If the paragraphs are double spaced, insert triple spacing between them.

► **Headings:** Like mini-essays, the separate sections of text should be labeled with meaningful titles that orient the reader. Ordinarily, a heading consists of a word or phrase, not a complete sentence (unless the heading is phrased as a question). Its position depends on its relative importance. A major heading is set in boldface capitals and centered,

LIKE THIS

A secondary heading is set either in uppercase letters or in both uppercase and lowercase, is flush with the left-hand margin, and can be set in boldface print,

LIKE THIS

or

Like This

A subtopic heading is run into the text, separated by a period or a colon, and is sometimes indented. Set in both uppercase and lowercase letters, it can be set in bold print, like the subtopic headings in this section.

These guidelines are flexible. Various approaches to heading design and placement are used, some of them quite elaborate. Perhaps the most helpful recommendation is that a report should use no more than three levels of heading. More than that, and the page or screen looks cluttered and confusing.

► **Lists:** Sometimes a vertical list is more effective than an actual paragraph. If the purpose of the list is to reveal a definite hierarchy of importance, the items in the list should be numbered in descending order, with the most important first and the least important last. Similarly, if the list's purpose is to reflect a chronological sequence, the items should be numbered in sequential order. Numbers are not necessary, however, in a list of approximately equal items. In those cases, *bullets* (solid black dots or arrows, like those throughout this book) will suffice

KINDS OF REPORTS

Like e-mails and letters, reports are written in all kinds of situations and for a wide range of purposes. Many reports are unique in the sense that they are written in response to one-time occurrences. On the other hand, it's not uncommon for a given report to be part of an ongoing series of weekly, monthly, or annual reports on the same subject. Among the most common categories of reports are the following:

► **Incident Report:** Explains the circumstances surrounding a troublesome occurrence such as an accident, fire, equipment malfunction, or security breach.
► **Progress Report:** Outlines the status of an ongoing project or undertaking.
► **Recommendation Report:** Urges that certain procedures be adopted (or rejected).
► **Travel Report:** Identifies the purpose and summarizes the results of business-related travel.
► **Lab Report:** Summarizes the circumstances, procedures, and results of an experiment or other laboratory-based activity.

Of course, any report can serve more than one purpose. An incident report, for example, may conclude with a recommendations section intended to minimize the likelihood of recurrence, as in the example that follows. But as in every writing situation, the writer of a report must consider the purpose and intended audience, and use an appropriate tone. The content, terminology, degree of detail, and formatting must be appropriate to the circumstances.

FALLKILL AUTOMOTIVE SERVICES

MEMORANDUM

DATE: October 13, 2017

TO: Bill Shorter
                   Business Office Manager

FROM: Frank Rodgers
                   Service Manager

SUBJECT: Incident Report

Brian Johnson, a technician in the service department, backed into and damaged a customer's vehicle in the parking lot last weekend.

DESCRIPTION OF INCIDENT

At approximately 12:15 on Saturday, October 7, Johnson was leaving the premises after completing his shift. A 2008 Jeep Cherokee belonging to a customer named Yuri Soupinski was parked in the lot, having been serviced by Johnson earlier in the day. Johnson failed to notice the Jeep and backed into it, damaging its bumper, headlights, and hood. Johnson immediately notified and apologized to the customer, who was less upset and more understanding than might be expected. Because Johnson was off the clock at the time of the accident, the company incurred no liability, and Johnson's own insurance (The Hartford) has initiated proceedings to resolve the matter. Soupinski was given a "loaner" vehicle, a 2014 Kia. He has expressed satisfaction with this arrangement, and his Jeep is now being repaired at Buzzy's Auto Body, a nearby shop selected by the Hartford.

RECOMMENDATIONS

► Because Johnson is a valued employee with no history of problems of any kind, no disciplinary action should be taken at this time.

► To minimize the likelihood of other occurrences of this nature, all personnel should be emphatically reminded to exercise extreme caution when moving customers' vehicles or their own.

► Management should convey formal apologies to Soupinski and perhaps offer him some sort of token compensation—a free oil change or some such—to ensure his continued good will and patronage.

CHECKLIST: SHORT REPORT

A good short report

- ▶ Follows memo or e-mail format

- ▶ Includes certain features:

     DATE line (appears automatically in e-mail)

     TO line, which provides the name (and, on memos, the title and/or department) of the intended recipient

     FROM line, which provides the name (appears automatically in e-mail) and, on a memo, the title and/or department of the sender; on a memo report, this line must be initialed by the sender before the report is sent

     SUBJECT line, which is a clear, accurate but brief statement of what the report is about; usually a word or short phrase is enough

- ▶ Is organized into separate, labeled sections covering the subject fully in logical sequence

- ▶ Uses clear, simple, straightforward language—nothing fancy

- ▶ Maintains an appropriate tone, neither too formal nor too conversational

- ▶ Employs effective visuals—tables, graphs, charts, and the like—where necessary to clarify content

- ▶ Contains no typos or mechanical errors in spelling, punctuation, or grammar

EXERCISES

1. Write a short report to the academic dean at your college, urging that a particular college policy be modified. Be specific about your reasons. Justify the change and provide concrete suggestions about possible alternative policies.

2. Write a short report to your English professor, outlining your progress in class. Begin with a statement of what you've learned and provide an objective assessment of your performance thus far, including attendance, grades, and any other pertinent information. Conclude with a realistic estimate of the final grade you anticipate receiving.

3. Write a short report to the student services director or the physical plant supervisor at your college, evaluating a major campus building with respect to accessibility to the physically challenged. Discuss the presence or absence of special signs, doors, ramps, elevators, restroom facilities, and the like. Suggest additional accommodations that should be provided if such needs exist.

4. Write a short report to your classmates in which you evaluate a nearby store that specializes in a particular product (for example, athletic shoes, books and music, or clothing). Discuss selection, quality, price, and service.

5. Write a short report to your classmates in which you compare two local restaurants featuring similar cuisine (for example, Chinese, Italian, or Middle Eastern). Discuss quality, atmosphere, price, and service.

CHAPTER 14

Proposals

LEARNING OBJECTIVES

When you complete this chapter, you will be able to

- ▶ Write both external and internal proposals, whether solicited or unsolicited
- ▶ Write proposals that include all the required elements of proposal content
- ▶ Write proposals that employ an appropriate tone for the audience

Like correspondence and reports, proposals are a major form of workplace writing and may also be assigned in college-level English courses. Simply defined, a proposal is a persuasive offer intended to secure authorization to perform a task or provide products or services that will benefit the reader. There are basically two kinds of proposals: solicited and unsolicited (that is, requested and unrequested). Like most other kinds of business writing, a proposal—solicited or not—may be either an external or in-house document.

EXTERNAL PROPOSALS

Solicited external proposals are written in response to an RFP (request for proposal) issued by a business, agency, or organization that has identified a situation or problem it wishes to address. The RFP spells out the details of the project (for example, providing structural upgrades to a building) and provides detailed instructions for submitting bids. Often quite lengthy and complex, they commonly appear in trade publications, as government releases, and on the web. Anyone wishing to compete for the contract must follow the stated guidelines exactly, creating a proposal that will convincingly demonstrate its superiority to the others received.

An unsolicited external proposal, on the other hand, originates with the writer, who has perceived the problem or need that the resulting proposal seeks to address. Writing such a proposal is more difficult than responding to an RFP because the writer must convince the reader that the problem exists and should be solved. In short, an unsolicited proposal—usually in the form of a business letter, perhaps accompanied by supporting materials—must be more strategically persuasive than a solicited proposal.

Whether solicited or unsolicited, however, every external proposal is motivated primarily by the desire for financial reimbursement, and—because it includes a summary of the writer's qualifications for the project—can almost be seen as a form of employment application.

INTERNAL PROPOSALS

Internal proposals are often rather short (usually in the form of an e-mail or memo report) because the writers and readers are already known to each other and the context is mutually understood. Solicited in-house proposals are not usually written in response to a formal RFP, but rather to a direct assignment from a manager, supervisor, or other administrator. Unsolicited in-house proposals are motivated by an employee's own perception of need—for example, the belief that a particular policy or procedure be adopted, modified, or abandoned.

ELEMENTS OF PROPOSALS

Irrespective of whether a proposal is external or internal, solicited or unsolicited, short or long, it should include certain elements, some of which may overlap:

- ▶ A clear summary of the situation or problem the proposal is addressing. If unsolicited, the proposal must convince the reader that there is in fact an important unmet need.
- ▶ A detailed explanation of how the proposal will correct the situation or problem. This is sometimes called the "project description."
- ▶ Confirmation of the project's feasibility and the anticipated benefits of completing it, as well as possible negative consequences of not doing so.
- ▶ Convincing refutation of any probable objections.
- ▶ Summary of the writer's credentials and qualifications for the project.
- ▶ Identification of any necessary resources, equipment, or support.
- ▶ A reliable timetable for completion of the project.
- ▶ An honest, itemized estimate of the costs. Deliberately understating the timeline or the budget is not only unethical but also fraudulent. Doing so can incur legal liability.
- ▶ A strong conclusion that will motivate the reader to accept the proposal. A convincing cost/benefit analysis is helpful here.

APPROPRIATE TONE

As emphasized throughout this book, all writing must be sensitive to considerations of purpose, audience, and tone. But this is especially important in proposal writing because of its fundamentally persuasive nature. A proposal writer must be alert to the differing requirements of upward, lateral, and downward communication (see Chapter 3). The phrasing should be reader-centered, using the "you" approach. And because proposals often seek to improve conditions by solving problems, it's important that they maintain a positive and upbeat tone. The writer must refrain from assigning blame for existing difficulties and should instead focus on solutions. This is especially important when writing in-house, where a hostile climate can result if a writer neglects to consider people's needs and feelings, particularly if the proposal's recommendations might increase or otherwise alter the responsibilities of co-workers.

Like any piece of writing, a proposal will be far more favorably received if well-written. Nothing tarnishes credibility faster than careless typos and basic errors in spelling, punctuation, and grammar. In addition, a proposal should be clear and well-organized. Further, the wording should be simple, direct, and concise, using active verbs and everyday vocabulary, with no rambling, wordy expression. As explained in Part 2, however, none of this can be achieved unless the writer employs the three-step approach: pre-writing, writing, and rewriting. The key is to revise, revise, and revise again. And proofread—carefully.

Here are two examples of well-executed proposals. The first, in letter format, is from a lawn care business offering its services to a local realty office. The second, in memo report format, is from a student to her instructor, regarding a topic for her research paper assignment.

ARDSLEY LAWNCARE
929 Alissa Road • Ardsley, WA 98100
(315) 555-1234

May 11, 2018

Jonathan Purdy
Purdy Realty
21 Bonita Avenue
Ardsley, WA 98100

Dear Mr. Purdy:

While servicing several properties in the vicinity of your business, we have noticed that your lawn might benefit from our attention, which would make your grounds even more attractive. Our proposal is as follows:

Five Lawn Treatments (Starting in Early Spring, Ending in Fall) @ $50 Each

- slow-release dry granular fertilizer
- pre-emergent crabgrass control
- balanced fertilizer
- broadleaf weed control
- surface insect control
- full clean-up after every treatment

We are a long-established, fully-insured local business offering free service calls and a "No Damage," money-back guarantee. We use only premium-quality, EPA-approved fertilizers and pesticides. (Please see enclosed brochure.)

Certainly any business such as yours always benefits greatly from projecting a highly professional image, and the appearance of the grounds surrounding your office is a key part of conveying that positive impression to potential clients.

If you wish to discuss our proposal, please contact us at your earliest convenience. We look forward to welcoming Purdy Realty as another satisfied Ardsley customer!

Sincerely,

Lauren Brooks

Lauren Brooks
Office Manager
(e-mail: lbrooks@ardsleylawncarecom)

Enclosure

Hoboken Community College
Hoboken, New Jersey 07030

PROPOSAL

DATE: 16 October 2017

TO: Professor Alan Shulman

FROM: Rosalie D'Elia, Student
             English 101 (Section 36)

SUBJECT: Research Paper Proposal

As you know, I'm pursuing an A.A.S. degree in Art History and am enrolled in your English Composition class. We have been assigned to submit a short proposal identifying our choice of topic for the research-based term paper due at the end of the semester. The proposal must include a brief outline, a preliminary bibliography of print sources, and a timeline for completion. Here's my proposal. I hope it's satisfactory.

Topic: Five Major Art Museums in New York City

Outline: Introduction
             1 – Frick Collection
             2 – Guggenheim
             3 – Metropolitan Museum of Art
             4 – Museum of Modern Art
             5 – Whitney Museum
             Conclusion

Preliminary
Bibliography: Anderson, Maxwell L. *American Visionaries: Selections from the Whitney Museum of American Art*. Whitney Museum of American Art, 2001.

Bailey, Colin B. *Building the Frick Collection: An Introduction to the House and Its Collections*. Frick Collection in Association with Scala, 2006.

Elderfield, John. *Modern Painting and Sculpture: 1880 to the Present at the Museum of Modern Art*. Museum of Modern Art, 2004.

The Metropolitan Museum of Art Guide. The Metropolitan Museum of Art, 2012.

MOMA Collection Highlights: 350 Works from the Museum of Modern Art. Museum of Modern Art, 2012.

Timeline: Oct. 23–Nov. 6: Research
              Nov. 26: Individual Conference
              Nov. 26-Dec. 4: Writing
              Dec. 5-9: Editing/Revising
              Dec. 10: Paper Due

My paper will focus on the history of each museum, along with its holdings and special features. Having personally visited each of these museums at least once during the past several years, I am well acquainted with the topic and can illustrate the paper with photos from my own collection. In addition, I have numerous brochures, flyers, and other materials that I can use—along with each museum's Web site—to supplement my preliminary bibliography.

Given my longtime interest in the subject, I'm confident I can do a good job with this topic, and I'm hoping you'll approve it. Please contact me if you need any further information. My student e-mail account is rdelia.stu@hcc.edu, and of course I can discuss this with you after class or during your office hours in Bradford Hall.

CHECKLIST: PROPOSAL

A good proposal

- ▶ Is prepared in a format (e-mail, memo, or letter) appropriate to the situation

- ▶ Clearly identifies the problem and fully explains how the proposal addresses it

- ▶ Confirms the feasibility of the proposal, refuting any probable objections and establishing the writer's credentials and qualifications for the project

- ▶ Provides a reliable timeline for completion of the project

- ▶ Identifies any necessary resources, equipment, or support, and includes an itemized budget

- ▶ Closes with a strong, persuasive conclusion that will motivate the reader to accept the proposal

- ▶ Uses clear, simple, straightforward language—nothing fancy

- ▶ Maintains an appropriate tone, neither too formal nor too conversational

- ▶ Employs effective visuals—tables, graphs, charts, and the like—where necessary to clarify content

- ▶ Contains no typos or mechanical errors in spelling, punctuation, or grammar

EXERCISES

1. Write a proposal seeking approval from your college's student activities director to create a new campus club or organization focused on an interest of yours.

2. Write a proposal to your college's athletic director to implement an addition or improvement to the intramural sports program.

3. Write a proposal seeking approval from the department head in your major field of study to take an elective course not among the program's recommended choices.

4. Write a proposal seeking approval from your workplace supervisor to implement a change in a particular policy or procedure you consider problematic.

5. Write a proposal seeking approval from your local library director to present a public lecture at the library on a topic you're knowledgeable about.

CHAPTER 15

Application Letters and Résumés

LEARNING OBJECTIVES

When you complete this chapter, you will be able to

- ▶ Write an effective job application letter using "full block" format and orderly, three-part organization to convey an accurate sense of your employment qualifications
- ▶ Write an effective job application letter that maintains an appropriately professional tone
- ▶ Design a visually attractive résumé that clearly details the several categories of information typically required by employers

Prepared in full block format and using three-part organization, a job application letter is in that sense no different from any other business letter. It should be neatly printed on 8½- by 11-inch white paper and framed by ample (1- to 1½-inch) margins. A job application letter is essentially a narrative summary of the applicant's qualifications, and in most cases should be no longer than one page. A résumé is a *detailed* list or outline of a job applicant's education, work history, and other credentials. It accompanies the application letter, complementing it by providing specifics about the information summarized in the letter. Although application letters and résumés are sometimes sent by traditional mail in response to job advertisements, many employers now prefer to receive them electronically, as e-mail attachments.

APPLICATION LETTER

When—as sometimes happens in job application situations—it's impossible to know the name of the person to whom you're writing, use "Dear Employer" as your salutation. This is a bit more original than such unimaginative greetings as the impersonal "To Whom It May Concern," the gender-biased "Dear Sir," or the old-fashioned "Dear Sir or Madam." And it will enable your letter to stand out from the others received, suggesting you're more resourceful than the other applicants.

Introduction

As explained in Chapter 12, the opening paragraph of any business letter creates context and states the letter's purpose. Since this is an employment application letter, you should say directly that you're applying for the job. Begin by coming right to the point, naming the position and how/where you heard about it. But start that first sentence with a descriptive phrase that creates context—and immediately gets the employer's attention—by identifying yourself as a qualified applicant, like this:

> As a recent County Community College graduate with an associate's degree in business, I am applying for the sales position described on your website.

Indeed, just one sentence like that would be enough as an opening paragraph.

Body Paragraphs

The middle section of any business letter must provide details. Accordingly, this is where you present a narrative summary of your qualifications: experience, education, and other credentials. Go into some depth, giving enough information to make the employer want to examine your résumé, which you should refer to specifically. But avoid *excessive* detail. Dates, addresses, and the like belong in the résumé, not the letter. Be sure to mention, however, any noteworthy attributes—specialized licenses, security clearances, computer skills, language fluency—that may set you apart from the competition. The purpose, of course, is to make the employer recognize your value as a prospective employee. Gear your letter accordingly. Without indulging in exaggeration or arrogant self-congratulation, explain why it would be in the employer's best interests to hire you. Sometimes a direct, straightforward statement such as this can be quite persuasive:

> With my college education now completed, I am eager to begin my career and will bring a
> high level of enthusiasm and commitment to this position.

Although there's no need to waste valuable résumé space listing references, you should mention in your letter that you can provide them. And you will be asked to do so if you become a finalist for the position. Therefore, when beginning your job search you'll need to find three people who are familiar with your work habits and are willing to write recommendation letters. Teachers and former employers are obvious possibilities. You must be certain, however, that anyone you choose will have nothing but good things to say. Tentative, halfhearted praise is worse than none at all. So you should ask to see a copy of any letter written on your behalf. Anyone reluctant to comply with such a request should almost certainly be replaced with someone more supportive.

Conclusion

The closing paragraph of any business letter, two or three sentences, just wraps things up, thanking the reader and providing a smooth conclusion that prevents the letter from ending abruptly. In an employment application letter this can be accomplished by mentioning that you're hoping for an interview. The fact is, nobody ever gets a job offer on the strength of a letter alone. The letter leads to the résumé, which (if you're lucky) leads to the interview, which (if you're *really* lucky) leads to a job offer. By mentioning the résumé and the interview in your letter, you reveal that you're a knowledgeable person familiar with the conventions of the hiring process.

Understand, however, that even one mechanical error in your letter may be enough to knock you out of the running. Make absolutely certain that there are no typos, spelling mistakes, faulty punctuation, or grammatical blunders—none whatsoever! Check and double-check to ensure that your letter (along with your résumé) is mechanically perfect. Here's an example of a good job application letter.

14 Broadman Parkway
Greenville, OR 97200
April 2, 2018

Ms. Carol Gagnon
Director of Human Resources
First National Bank of Greenville
925 Greenville Boulevard
Greenville, OR 97200

Dear Ms. Gagnon:

As an honor student about to graduate from County Community College with an AAS degree in Banking and Finance, I am applying for the teller trainee position advertised in *The Greenville Daily Sentinel.*

In college I have maintained a 3.8 grade-point average while serving as vice-president of the Mathematics Club and treasurer of the Asian-American Students Union. In keeping with my ongoing commitment to community service, last summer I joined a group of County Community College students working with senior citizens at the Greenville Acres Nursing Home, where we showed the residents how to create social media Web sites. My academic training, hands-on knowledge gained from extracurricular activities, and enhanced interpersonal skills acquired at Greenville Acres—not to mention my language skills in Korean and Spanish—equip me to become a valued member of your staff. Past and current employers, listed on the enclosed résumé, will attest to my strong work ethic. I can provide those individuals' names and contact information on request.

Thank you for considering my application. Please phone or e-mail me to arrange an interview at your convenience.

Sincerely,

Dustin Kim

Dustin Kim

Enclosure: résumé

RÉSUMÉ

As mentioned earlier, a résumé is a detailed listing of the job applicant's qualifications. The following categories of information typically appear:

- ► Contact Information
- ► Career Objective
- ► Education
- ► Work Experience
- ► Military Service
- ► Computer Literacy
- ► Specialized Skills or Credentials
- ► Honors and Awards
- ► Community Service

Of course, few résumés include *all* these categories. Not everyone has served in the military, for example, or received awards. Not everyone is active in the community or possesses special skills. But practically anyone can create an effective résumé. The trick is to carefully evaluate your background and emphasize your strengths. A person with a college degree but little work experience, for example, would highlight the education component. On the other hand, someone whose job experience outweighed the schooling would emphasize the employment history. Here are some pointers regarding the various sections of a résumé.

Contact Information

Provide *only* your name, address, phone number, and e-mail address, all at the top of the page. Note: If your e-mail address is in any way silly or juvenile, you must establish a professional e-mail account for job-search purposes. Ditto for your voice mail message. (And if your Facebook or other social networking sites contain anything that might displease potential employers, that must also be corrected.)

Career Objective

A brief but focused statement of your professional goals. Of course, if you wind up applying for a broad range of positions, this section must be revised to suit each situation.

Education

Using *reverse* chronological order (most recent first), provide the name and address of each school you've attended, and mention your program(s) of study and any degrees, diplomas, certificates, or honors received. Omit high school unless you're trying to beef up an otherwise skimpy résumé.

Work Experience

Like the education section, this is one of the most important parts of your résumé. Again using reverse chronological order, provide each job title, dates of employment, name and address of employer, and—if they're not obvious from the job title—the principal duties involved. If you've worked at many different jobs, some for short periods, it's wise to list only your most important positions and lump the others together in a one-sentence summary like this:

> Have also held part-time and temporary positions as a farm worker, retail sales clerk, and marina dock attendant.

Notice that in résumé writing it's not necessary to say "I." You are allowed to save space by using a somewhat telegraphic style that cuts right to the verb: "Did this, did that," rather than "I did this, I did that."

Military Service

If applicable, list the branch and dates of service, the highest rank achieved, and any noteworthy travel or duty. Applicants with no other significant employment history sometimes list military service under the work experience category.

Computer Literacy

A highly valued attribute—indeed, a necessary one—in today's technology-driven workplace. Mention specific word-processing and other software with which you're familiar (for example, Microsoft Word and Excel or Adobe Photoshop).

Specialized Skills or Credentials

Include licenses, certifications, security clearances, language competency, and proficiency with specific machines—in short, any "plus" that doesn't fit neatly elsewhere.

Honors and Awards

These can be academic or otherwise. In some cases—if you received a medal while in the military, for example, or made the college honor roll—it's best to include such distinctions under the appropriate categories. But if the Kiwanis Club awarded you its annual scholarship or you were cited for community leadership by the mayor, these honors would be highlighted in a separate category.

Community Service

Volunteer work or memberships in local clubs, organizations, or church groups are appropriate here. Most helpful are well-known activities such as Scouting, Little League, 4-H, and the like. Include details: dates of service or membership, offices held, special projects you initiated or coordinated. But don't claim involvement in organizations or activities you actually know little about. Such unethical falsification will become obvious if the interviewer asks about your outside interests.

As we have seen, all business letters—application letters included—are governed by standards that determine layout and organization: full block style, three-part structure. Once you understand those guidelines, writing a letter is really pretty easy. But résumés are another story. Many different approaches are in widespread use, and the design and appearance of a résumé are entirely up to the person writing it. This is good and bad. On the "plus" side, this flexibility gives the writer a great deal of freedom to experiment and innovate. On the "minus" side, however, this liberty often results in résumés that are visually cluttered and hard to read. To avoid that pitfall, follow these well-established guidelines:

- ► Like the application letter, the résumé should be printed on 8½- by 11-inch white paper, with ample margins. Use boldface, underlining, bullets, and other design options to create an inviting appearance. But don't overdo it. Use no more than two different fonts and three different type sizes.
- ► The various categories of information must be clearly labeled and distinct from one another so the employer can quickly review your background without having to labor over the page or screen. Indeed, most employers will simply discard a confusing résumé and move on to the next one.

► All necessary details must appear—names, addresses, dates, and so on—and must be presented in a uniform format throughout. For example, do not abbreviate words like *Avenue* and *Street* in one section and then spell them out elsewhere. Be consistent.

► Use *reverse* chronological order; list the most recent information first, then work backward through time.

► Do not allow your résumé to exceed two pages.

► Like your letter, your résumé must be mechanically perfect, with no errors in spelling, punctuation, or grammar. Carefully edit for careless blunders—typos, inconsistent spacing, and the like.

What follows is a sample résumé that observes the basic principles of good design. Prepared in standard, reverse-chronological format, it would accompany the letter shown earlier.

Dustin Kim

14 Broadman Parkway, Greenville OR 97200
(202) 556-2557 • dkim@cccstudent.edu

Career Objective

Secure, full-time position in banking.

Education

County Community College (2014–present)
1101 College Drive, Greenville OR

Will graduate in May 2018 with AAS degree in Banking and Finance. Have maintained 3.80 grade point average while serving as vice-president of the Mathematics Club and treasurer of the Asian-American Students Union.

Experience

- Counter Clerk (2015–present)
  Quik Stop Grocery, 34 Wade Street, Greenville OR

  Part-time position to help meet college expenses.

- Warehouse Worker (2012–2013)
  Cantor & Mitchell, Inc., 1 Meeker Avenue, Greenville OR

  Full-time job after high school, before deciding to pursue college education.

Language Proficiency

- Native fluency in Korean

- Conversational ability in Spanish (two years of college-level coursework)

Community Activities

- Volunteer, Greenville Acres Nursing Home (Summer, 2015)
  Taught computer skills (Facebook, etc.) to senior citizens.

- Assistant Baseball Coach, Greenville Little League (2016–present)

CHECKLIST: APPLICATION LETTER & RESUME

A good application letter

- ▶ Follows full block format

- ▶ Is organized into paragraphs

    First paragraph asks for the job by name and indicates where you learned of the opening

    Middle paragraphs briefly outline your credentials and refer the reader to your résumé

    Last paragraph politely achieves closure, mentioning that you would like an interview

- ▶ Does not exceed one page

- ▶ Uses clear, simple, straightforward language—nothing fancy

- ▶ Maintains an appropriate tone, neither too formal nor too conversational

- ▶ Contains no typos or mechanical errors in spelling, punctuation, or grammar

A good résumé

- ▶ *Looks* good, making effective use of white space, capitalization, bold print, and other format options

- ▶ Includes no irrelevant personal information

- ▶ Includes separate, labeled sections for education, experience, and other major categories of professional qualifications, providing all necessary details (dates, addresses, etc.)

- ▶ Maintains a consistent approach to abbreviation, spacing, and other design elements

- ▶ Does not exceed one page

- ▶ Contains no typos or mechanical errors

EXERCISES

Three application letters accompanied by résumés follow. For a variety of reasons, all are badly flawed. Rewrite each to eliminate its particular weaknesses.

Jennifer Reaney
333 Fairmount Ave.
Jersey City, N.J. 03506
November 10, 2017

Mr. Morton Higgins
Glenwood Restaurant
144 West Side Avnue
Jersey City, New Jersey

Dear Sir;

I saw your add in The Jersey Journal and want to apply for the job.

I have inclosed my resume, I have all the qualifications for which you are looking for.

I look forward to hearing from you soon.

Your's truley,

Jennifer Reaney

RESUME

Name: Jennifer Reaney
Address: 333 Fairmount Ave.
Jersey City, New Jersey
Phone: (201) 333–1234
Religion: Cathlic
Date of Birth: January 10, 1993

Marital Status: divorced, two kids
Health: Excellent
Height: 5"3'
Weight: 155 lbs
Citizenship: U.S.A.
Military Service: none

Education

2017 to now	New Jersey City University Hospitality Manigemint Major
Class of 2011	Dickinson High School Jersey City, N.J.

Experience

20011	Dishwasher Mama Gina's Ristorante Jersey City, New Jersey
2012	Waitress Tania's Restaurant Jersey City, N.J.
2013	Dishwasher Pete & Dominics Restaurant Jersey City, NJ
20013–201	Waitress Pete & Dominic's Restaurant Jersey City, N.J.
2014	Hostess Pete and Dominics Jersey City, N.J.
2015–2016	Bartender Churchills Tavern Bayonne New Jersey
2016–now	Dining Room Manger Churchills Bayonne, NJ

Computers

I know how to use the POSiTouch computer systems.

References—Excelent refrences available on request

385 Leslie Street
Wallach, CA 92500
November 10, 2017

Ms. Mary Jane Reed, Branch Manager
Central Bank of Wallach
Wallach, CA 92500

Dear Ms. Reed:

As a May 2017 graduate of County Community College with an A.A.S. degree and a dual major
in Business and Accounting, I am very much interested in the financial services position you have
advertised in the November 6 edition of *The Smallville Courier*, and I would like you to consider me a
serious candidate for that opening.

As mentioned above, I am a 2017 graduate of County Community College with an A.A.S. degree
and a dual major in Business and Accounting, and I was on either the Dean's List (honors) or the
President's List (high honors) every semester, compiling an overall GPA (grade-point average) of 3.87
and earning admission to the prestigious Phi Theta Kappa honor society. I completed such challenging
classes as Business Law, Economics, Computer Applications, Principles of Management, Financial
Management, Business Math, and Investment Science, along with General Education requirements
such as English 101 & 102, Social Science (Psychology and Sociology), Lab Science (Biology 1 & 2),
and Physical Education (Physical Fitness and First Aid), and several electives. While at CCC I served
as Student Congress Treasurer for two semesters, maintaining a $3000 budget that funded thirty-five
campus organizations; it was my responsibility to approve and verify all disbursements, including the
Student Congress payroll. I also competed on the varsity tennis team during my second year, playing in
both singles and doubles matches, compiling a 6 & 2 singles record and a 4 & 3 doubles record as the
team achieved a winning season. In addition, I also completed an internship at the Sterling Insurance
Company in nearby Elliston, California during the fall semester of 2016, contacting and meeting
with prospective clients, answering client inquiries, and performing general office duties. During the
summers of 2016, 2015, and 2014 I worked as a Trust Administrative Assistant at the First City Bank
of Elliston, researching financial investment data, organizing trust account information, screening and
answering customer inquiries, and composing routine business correspondence. Further, I was named
the 2016 Red Cross "Volunteer of the Year" for this region.

Obviously, I am very highly qualified for the position you have advertised, and I can provide excellent
references upon request. I look forward to meeting with you in an interview setting at your very earliest
convenience. Thank you very much for considering me for this highly desirable position.

Sincerely,

Alexander Portnoy

Résumé

Alexander Portnoy
385 Leslie Street
Wallach, CA 92500
(805) 555-5555
Aportnoy2@email.net

OBJECTIVE
A permanent position in financial services.

EDUCATION
Associate in Applied Science
County Community College

EXPERIENCE
Student Congress Treasurer
County Community College
Intern

Sterling Insurance Company

Trust Administrative Assistant
First City Bank of Elliston

INTERESTS
Tennis

REFERENCES
Available upon request.

April 25, 2018

Shaniqua Gaines
Director of Security
Chesterton Mall
Chesterton, OH 44300

Dear Mrs. Gaines:

I will be graduating from college with a Certificate in Security Management next month, and would like to apply for the shopping center security position you have announced. My background—especially my education, my military service as an M.P., and my former employment as a college campus security guard—makes me well-qualified for this job. After you have had some time to review my enclosed resume I will contact you about arranging an interview.

Thank you,

Neil E. Whalen

Neil E. Whalen

RESUME

NAME: Neil E. Whalen

ADDRESS: 409 Kahler Road
                         Chesterton, OH 90406

PHONE: (805) 123-1234

CAREER OBJECTIVE: Full-Time Position as a Shopping Mall Security Guard

EDUCATION: Certificate in Security Management (2018)
                         John Jay College
                         New York, NY

EMPLOYMENT: Stockbroker's Assistant (2010–2012)
                         Carlisle & Jacquelin
                         2 Broadway
                         New York, NY 10005

RESPONSIBILITIES: Worked with stockbrokers on the trading floor of the New York Stock
                         Exchange, executing "odd lot" market orders.

EMPLOYMENT: Military Policeman (2012–2014)
                         United States Army War College
                         Carlisle Barracks
                         Carlisle, PA 17013

RESPONSIBILITIES: Performed such duties as radio car patrol, traffic control, and building security,
                         checking top-secret security passes.

EMPLOYMENT: Campus Security Officer (2014–2016)
                         County Community College
                         1101 College Drive
                         Binghamton, MO 64100

RESPONSIBILITIES: Enforced parking regulations, checked student i.d., monitored campus for
                         safety and security violations.

INTERESTS & ACTIVITIES: sports, martial arts, hunting

REFERENCES: None at present.

PART 6

Research-Based Writing

In most college courses (and in many high school classes as well), students are required to complete one or more research-based writing assignments. Sometimes the topic is given by the teacher, but at the college level students are often permitted to choose. In either case, you have to gather information by consulting reliable sources: books, magazines, newspapers, academic journals, and websites. But you can't simply copy other writers' ideas word-for-word and present them as if they were your own. That's plagiarism. Instead, you're required to use summary, paraphrase, and quotation correctly, and provide documentation to identify your sources and indicate where you've used them. In addition, research-based assignments sometimes involve writing collaboratively. These chapters show you how to handle all these aspects of research-based writing.

CHAPTER 16

Finding, Evaluating, and Integrating Sources of Information

LEARNING OBJECTIVES

When you complete this chapter, you will be able to

- ▶ Distinguish between reliable and unreliable sources of information
- ▶ Integrate information by using summary, paraphrase, and quotation correctly
- ▶ Function productively in collaborative writing situations

Whether your professor assigns the topic of your research or allows you to select your own, you have to conduct research that enables you to gather enough information to cover the topic in depth, going beyond what you already know about it.

SOURCES

The basic sources of information appropriate for use in research-based writing are books, magazines, newspapers, academic journals, and websites.

Books

The most traditional source of in-depth information, books are published on an enormous range of topics. Whatever you're writing about, there are countless books that can provide you with abundant material that can enable you to develop your paper. But always look for books that have been published fairly recently. This helps you narrow your focus when searching your college library's holdings. More importantly, the recent titles are the most up-to-date and therefore reflect current thinking on the topic. In addition, it makes sense to choose books from university presses and long-established commercial publishers because these are more selective in choosing what to print. As a result, their books tend to be more accurate and reliable than those produced by lesser-known publishers. Here are a half-dozen of the most highly-regarded commercial houses, all based in New York:

- ▶ Farrar, Straus, and Giroux
- ▶ Harper Collins
- ▶ Houghton Mifflin
- ▶ Alfred A. Knopf
- ▶ W.W. Norton & Company
- ▶ Random House

Magazines

Even a brief glance at the display of magazines in any store that sells them reveals that countless such periodicals are published on a weekly or monthly basis. Some, like *Time* and *Sports Illustrated*, are quite well-known, others less so. But the mere fact that a magazine enjoys high visibility does not necessarily mean it's a good source. Many popular magazines are quite superficial, devoted to coverage of celebrity gossip and other trivial concerns. There are also many good but highly specialized magazines (like *Car & Driver*, *Psychology Today*, and *Wired*) that focus exclusively on one area of interest. Others, however, have broader appeal. Here's a short list of some of the best general audience magazines, all of which cover the arts and current events:

- ▶ *The Atlantic*
- ▶ *The Economist*
- ▶ *Harper's*
- ▶ *The Nation*
- ▶ *The New Republic*
- ▶ *The New Yorker*

Most college and university libraries maintain subscriptions to these magazines, along with many others. But it's advisable to check with your professor before using magazines as sources because some consider them too lightweight for serious research and will not accept them.

Newspapers

Although several major American newspapers have gone out of business in recent years, there are literally hundreds still being published. But only a few are typically cited as sources in academic writing. Here's the list, a short one:

- ▶ *The Los Angeles Times*
- ▶ *The Wall Street Journal*
- ▶ *The New York Times*
- ▶ *The Washington Post*

The New York Times and *The Washington Post* (not to be confused with the tabloid-format *New York Post*) are considered the most reputable. Indeed, *The New York Times* is one of the most respected newspapers not only in this country but in the world. Virtually all college and university libraries subscribe to *The New York Times* and *The Wall Street Journal*, along with local papers, and may maintain microfilm files going back many years. In addition, there are web archives that provide access to past issues.

Academic Journals

Every area of academic study supports many scholarly journals that publish highly specialized articles, almost always written by professors who teach in that field. Accordingly, these essays often discuss recent research or newly emerging theories. Given their familiarity with these journals, many professors require their students to consult such sources when completing research-based assignments.

Databases

To track down journal articles (or, for that matter, articles in magazines and newspapers as well), it's easiest to consult computerized databases that allow you to locate material related to your topic. Here are several very useful such resources, all available online from EBSCOhost, a service subscribed to by college and university libraries:

- ▶ **Academic Search Complete** is the most comprehensive database, covering articles in thousands of publications in all disciplines.
- ▶ **Associates Program Source** is geared to the needs of community college students, focusing on nearly 1,000 journals aligned with programs of study typical of the two-year schools.
- ▶ **Business Source Complete** is devoted exclusively to indexing and abstracts of business articles as far back as the 1880s.
- ▶ **CINAHL Plus with Full Text** is the best database for articles about nursing and allied health services, covering more than 750 scholarly journals in those fields.
- ▶ **Computer Source** provides up-to-date information on articles about trends and developments in the field of high technology.
- ▶ **ERIC** is the Education Resource Information Center database, containing links to more than 300,000 articles dating back to the 1960s.
- ▶ **GreenFILE** covers the environment, with information on nearly 5,000 articles about global warming, green building, pollution, sustainable agriculture, renewable energy, recycling, and the like.
- ▶ **Humanities International Complete** includes data on more than 2,000 journals devoted to the humanities (art, music, literature, film, etc.)
- ▶ **Newspaper Source Plus** covers more than 700 newspapers along with more than a half-million television and radio news transcripts.
- ▶ **Vocational and Career Collection** serves community colleges and trade schools by providing information on articles in more than 300 trade and industry-related periodicals.

Websites

As anyone who has ever clicked a mouse has immediately discovered, the amount of information available on the web is seemingly unlimited. A Google search for virtually any topic results in hundreds if not thousands of results. But the quality of this material varies greatly. The seventh edition of the *MLA Handbook for Writers of Research Papers* says it quite well:

> Assessing Internet resources is a particular challenge. Whereas the print publications that researchers depend on are generally issued by reputable publishers, like university presses, that accept responsibility for the quality and reliability of the works they distribute, relatively few electronic publications currently have comparable authority. Some Internet publications are peer-reviewed, but others are not. Online materials are often self-published, without any outside review. (34)

Therefore, you must be very selective when gathering information online. Here are some questions to ask yourself when evaluating electronic sources:

- ▶ Who has posted or sponsored this site? An individual? An organization? A special interest or advocacy group? What are their credentials or qualifications? The final suffix in the URL will reveal a site's origins:

.com	commercial enterprise
.org	nonprofit organization
.edu	college, university, or other educational institution
.gov	government agency
.mil	military group

- ▶ Sometimes it's helpful to enter the individual's or group's name in a search engine to see what other sites emerge. This can reveal affiliations and biases that have an impact on credibility.
- ▶ Does the site itself provide links to related sites? Does it credit its own sources?
- ▶ Is the information presented in a reasonably objective fashion or does the site seem to favor or promote a particular viewpoint or perspective?
- ▶ Does the site provide an e-mail address or other contact information that you can use to seek more background?
- ▶ What is the date of the posting? Is the information current?
- ▶ How well-written is the site? How well designed? In short, does it seem to be the work of amateurs or professionals?

Be aware that, despite its wide range and resulting popularity among Internet users, *Wikipedia, the free encyclopedia* is not considered an acceptable source for academic research. For that matter, most professors do not accept print encyclopedias either. But encyclopedias—*Wikipedia* included—can lead you to more highly regarded sources because encyclopedia entries commonly include a bibliography of related works.

INTEGRATING INFORMATION

When developing your paper by inserting information you've gathered from your research, there are basically three approaches you can use: summary, paraphrase, and quotation. Most research-based writing relies on all three. But they are quite different from one another.

Summary

In the very broadest sense, all writing is a form of summary. Whenever we put words on paper or computer screen, we condense ideas and information to make them clear to the reader. Ordinarily, however, the term *summary* refers to a brief but accurate statement of the essential content of something heard, seen, or read. For any kind of summary, the writer reduces a body of material to its bare essentials. Summarizing is therefore an exercise in compression, requiring simple and concrete language. Summarizing requires an especially keen sense not only of what to include, but also what to *leave out*. The goal is to highlight key points and not burden the reader with unnecessary details. Because of its innately compact nature, a summary is always a shorter version of the original wording. If any original wording is retained, it must be enclosed in quotation marks. (See "Quotation," below.)

Paraphrase

Like summary, paraphrase involves rewording. But, *unlike* summary, it's often *longer* than the original. That's because its purpose is not only to present the original information but also to clarify it. Sometimes this is accomplished by choosing words that are more familiar. Often it involves providing explanations or re-sequencing the original information to make it easier to understand. Paraphrase is especially useful when you're attempting to deal with technical or otherwise specialized subject matter.

Quotation

Sometimes called "direct quotation," this involves using the exact same phrasing that appears in the original, repeating it *verbatim* (word-for-word), and enclosing it within quotation marks. Indeed, that's the main purpose of quotation marks—to indicate that what appears between them is an exact copy. Sometimes a quotation will include *ellipses* (four periods). They indicate that an entire sentence or more has been removed from the original at that point. When something is removed *within* a quoted sentence, the ellipsis consists of only three periods.

If you wish to use a longer, paragraph-length quotation, you can insert it into your paper using "block" quotation, as in the example below, a passage from *New York Safe Boating*, a publication of the New York State Office of Parks, Recreation and Historic Preservation:

> The standard outboard engine is a complete propulsion unit. Boats that use outboard engines don't have rudders, so the boat turns in response to operator's turning of the outboard engine. Most outboard engines are mounted on the transom of the boat. The outboard engine has many advantages. In general, outboards have an excellent power to weight ratio so the operator can get a lot of power and speed out of a small engine. These engines are easy to service and replace. They don't take up space in the boat, leaving more room for passengers and gear. On the downside, they are not as efficient or economical to operate as other types of engines. (9)

Note that block quotation does not require quotation marks. This is because the block format itself indicates that the passage is a quote. Although quotation certainly has value, not least because it exactly captures the content and tone of the source, do not depend on it too heavily. Good research-based writing is never simply an exercise in stringing quotes together. No more than 20 percent of your paper should consist of quotation.

COLLABORATION

Most writing is done by one person working alone. This is true of e-mail, business letters, short reports, and certainly the academic essay. And it's often true of long papers as well. However, since the subject matter of long papers is usually complex, they are sometimes group-written. Indeed, most college students—and nearly all workplace writers—are called upon to cooperate on writing projects at least occasionally. This kind of teamwork is common because it affords certain real advantages.

For example, a group that works well together can produce a long paper faster than one person working alone. In addition, a team possesses a broader perspective and greater range of knowledge and expertise than an individual. To slightly amend the old saying, two heads—or more—are better than one. In addition, with the increasing sophistication of groupware (word-processing and document design programs created specifically for collaborative use) such as Google Docs, teamworking has become easier and faster than ever.

Nevertheless, collaboration can pose problems if the members of the group have difficulty interacting smoothly. Teamwork requires everyone involved to exercise tact, courtesy, and responsibility. The following factors are essential to successful collaboration:

1. Everyone on the team must fully understand the purpose, goals, and intended audience of the project.

2. Team members must agree to set aside individual preferences in favor of the group's collective judgment.

3. The team must have a leader—someone whom the other members are willing to recognize as the coordinator. Ideally, the leader is elected from within the group, rather than self-appointed. The leader must not only be knowledgeable and competent, but should also be a "people person" with good interpersonal skills. The leader has many responsibilities:

   ▶ Helps establish procedural guidelines, especially regarding progress assessment
   ▶ Monitors team members' involvement, providing encouragement and assistance
   ▶ Promotes consensus and referees disagreements
   ▶ Maintains an accurate master file of the evolving document

   In short, the leader functions as team manager, ensuring a successful outcome by keeping everyone on task and holding the whole effort together.

4. The team must create clearly defined roles for the other members, assigning responsibilities according to everyone's talents and strengths. For example, the group's most competent researcher takes charge of information retrieval. Someone trained in drafting or computer-assisted design agrees to format the report and create visuals. The member with the best keyboarding skills actually produces the document. The best writer is the overall editor, making final judgments on matters of organization, style, mechanics, and the like. If an oral presentation is required, the group's most confident public speaker assumes that responsibility. In some cases a given individual might play more than one role, but everyone must feel satisfied that the work has been fairly distributed.

5. Once the project has begun, the team continuously assesses its progress, prevents duplication of effort, and resolves any problems that may arise. All disagreements or differences of opinion are reconciled in a productive manner. In any group undertaking, a certain amount of conflict is inevitable and indeed necessary to achieve consensus. This interplay, however, should be a source of creative energy, not antagonism. Issues must be dealt with on an objectively intellectual level, not in a personal or emotional manner.

6. All members of the group must complete their fair share of the work in a conscientious manner and observe all deadlines. Nothing is more disruptive to a team's progress than an irresponsible member who fails to complete work punctually or "vanishes" for long periods of time. To maintain contact, group members should exchange phone numbers and/or e-mail addresses. Another option is to use file transfer protocol (FTP) to create a common website to which group members can post drafts for review by their teammates. In any case, electronic communication should be seen simply as a way to keep in touch, not as a substitute for frequent face-to-face interaction.

Theoretically, a group can handle the actual writing of the paper in one of three ways:

► The whole team writes the paper collectively, then the editor revises the draft and submits it to the group for final approval or additional revisions.
► One person writes the entire paper, and then the group—led by the editor—revises it collectively.
► Each team member writes one part of the paper individually, and then the editor revises each part and submits the complete draft to the whole group for final approval or additional revisions.

Of these alternatives, the first is the most truly collaborative but is also extremely difficult and time-consuming, requiring exceptional harmony within the group. The second method is preferable but places too great a burden on one writer. The third approach is the most common and is certainly the best, provided the editor seeks clarification from individuals whenever necessary during the editing process. For this reason, the third approach is the one that underlies most of what's been said here. Note, however, that in all three approaches the whole group gets to see the proposed final version and provide additional fine-tuning if necessary. In the workplace, everybody on the team will be equally responsible for the outcome. And in the college setting, everybody usually receives the same grade on the assignment. Therefore, no one should be dissatisfied with the final product. Collaboration is, after all, a team effort with the goal of producing a polished document approved by all members of the team.

EXERCISES

1. Pretend you are writing a research paper on the topic of cigarette smoking among doctors and nurses. Using your college library's resources and the Internet, track down five sources of information on this subject:

   ▶ a chapter in an edited book

   _____

   ▶ an article in a popular magazine

   _____

   ▶ an article in a medical journal

   _____

   ▶ an article in a major newspaper

   _____

   ▶ a discussion on a website

   _____

2. Find an obviously biased (and therefore unreliable) website devoted to a controversial topic such as gun control, global warming, or capital punishment. Write a short explanation of why you think the site is questionable.

   _____

   _____

   _____

3. Find an apparently objective (and therefore reliable) website devoted to a controversial topic such as those mentioned in Exercise 2. Write a short explanation of why you think the site is legitimate.

   _____

   _____

   _____

4. Write a summary of the Gettysburg Address.

5. Write a paraphrase of the Gettysburg Address.

6. Team up with two or three other students and produce a detailed list of the classrooms, labs, and other instructional spaces in one campus building. Be sure to include the location of each, along with all furnishings and equipment (e.g., computers, projectors, interactive whiteboards, etc.). Then write a collaborative essay in which you discuss whether the building is well suited to its purposes.

CHAPTER 17

Documentation

LEARNING OBJECTIVES

When you complete this chapter, you will be able to

- ▶ Avoid plagiarism
- ▶ Create correctly formatted bibliographies using both MLA and APA styles
- ▶ Create correct in-text citations using both MLA and APA styles

Whatever sources you finally use in a research assignment, you must provide documentation. That is, you must identify those sources and indicate where you have used them. In everyday writing this is often accomplished by inserting the relevant information directly into the text, as in this example.

> As journalist Verlyn Klinkenborg says in his article "How to Destroy Species, Including Us," in the March 20, 2014, issue of *The New York Review of Books*, "The last time species died out as fast as they're doing now was 65 million years ago, when an asteroid crashed into earth at a low angle, leaving an enormous crater near what is now the Yucatán and causing a long-lasting global winter."

This straightforward approach eliminates the need for a bibliography (list of sources) at the end of the piece. In academic writing, however, documentation nearly always includes both a bibliography and parenthetical citations identifying the origin of each quotation, statistic, paraphrase, or visual when it appears within the text.

PLAGIARISM

Documentation is necessary to avoid *plagiarism*, which the new (eighth) edition of the *MLA Handbook* defines as, "presenting another person's ideas, information, expressions, or entire work as one's own...a kind of fraud...always a serious moral and ethical offense" (7). The previous (seventh) edition of the *Handbook* provided useful guidelines for recognizing and avoiding plagiarism:

> "You have plagiarized if:

- ▶ you took notes that did not distinguish summary and paraphrase from quotation and then you presented wording from the notes as if it were all your own.
- ▶ while browsing the Web, you copied text and pasted it into your paper without quotation marks or without citing the source.

- you repeated or paraphrased someone's wording without acknowledgment.
- you took someone's unique or particularly apt phrase without acknowledgment.
- you paraphrased someone's argument or presented someone's line of thought without acknowledgment.
- you bought or otherwise acquired a research paper and handed in part or all of it as your own.

You can avoid plagiarism by:

- making a list of the writers and viewpoints you discovered in your research and using this list to double-check the presentation of material in your paper.
- keeping the following three categories distinct in your notes: your ideas, your summaries of others' material, and exact wording you copy.
- identifying the sources of all material you borrow—exact wording, paraphrases, ideas, arguments, and facts.
- checking with your instructor when you are uncertain about your use of sources." (*MLA Handbook for Writers of Research Papers*, 7th ed., pp. 60–61)

BIBLIOGRAPHY

When creating the list of sources that must appear at the end of your paper, you are expected to use one of the established formats. The MLA format, which titles the list "Works Cited," and the American Psychological Association (APA) format, which titles the list "References," are the most commonly taught in college courses, although a great many others do exist: American Chemical Society (ACS), American Institute of Physics (AIP), American Mathematical Society (AMS), the Council of Biology Editors (CBE), and the format described in *The Chicago Manual of Style* (sometimes referred to as "Turabian," after Kate L. Turabian, the University of Chicago secretary who wrote the first version of the manual in the 1930s), to name just a few. Here is a typical bibliography entry formatted according to MLA and APA guidelines:

> **MLA**   Standage, Tom. *Writing on the Wall: Social Media—the First 2,000 Years*. Bloomsbury, 2013.

> **APA**   Standage, T. (2013). *Writing on the wall: Social media—the first 2,000 years*. New York: Bloomsbury.

Notice the differences between the two formats. Perhaps the most obvious is the placement of the publication date. But variations also exist with respect to capitalization, punctuation, and abbreviation. In both systems, however, double-spacing is used throughout, and book titles—like those of newspapers, magazines, journals, and other periodicals—are italicized. In both formats, entries appear in alphabetical order by authors' last names or, for anonymous works, by the first significant word in the title.

There are many other kinds of sources besides single-author books, however, and each requires a slightly different handling. Here are some of the most common citations:

Book by Two Authors

> **MLA**   Singer, P.W. and Allan Friedman. *Cybersecurity and Cyberwar: What Everyone Needs to Know*. Oxford UP, 2014.

> **APA**   Singer, P.W., & Friedman, A. (2014). *Cybersecurity and cyberwar: What everyone needs to know*. New York: Oxford University.

Book by Three or More Authors

MLA   Galloway, Alexander G., et al. *Excommunication: Three Inquiries in Media and Mediation.* U of Chicago P, 2013.

APA   Galloway, A. G., Thacker, E., & Wark, M. (2013). *Excommunication: Three inquiries in media and mediation.* University of Chicago.

Book by a Collective Author

MLA   *Soares Book on Grounding and Bonding.* 11th ed. International Association of Electrical Inspectors, 2011.

APA   International Association of Electrical Inspectors (2011). *Soares book on grounding and bonding.* (11th ed.). Richardson, TX: Author.

Edited Book of Articles

MLA   Snickars, Pelle and Patrick Vonderau, editors. *The IPhone and the Future of Media.* Columbia UP, 2012.

APA   Snickars, P. & Vonderau, P. (eds.). (2012). *The iPhone and the future of media.* New York: Columbia University.

Chapter in an Edited Book

MLA   Conley, Dalton. "The End of Solitude." *The iPhone and the Future of Media,* edited by Pelle Snickars and Patrick Vonderau, Columbia UP, 2012.

APA   Conley, D. (2012). The end of solitude. In P. Snickars & P. Vonderau (Eds.), *The iPhone and the future of media* (pp. 311–316). New York: Columbia University.

Article in a Newspaper

MLA   Mouawad, Jad. "JetBlue Airways' Pilots Vote to Join Union." *The New York Times,* 23 Apr. 2014, p. B2.

APA   Mouawad, J. (2014, April 23). JetBlue airways' pilots vote to join union. *The New York Times,* p. B5.

Anonymous Article in a Newspaper

MLA   "Motorcycle Crashes Cost $16 Billion Annually." *The Wall Street Journal,* 28 Nov. 2012, p. 47.

APA   Motorcycle crashes cost $16 billion annually (2012, November 28). *The Wall Street Journal,* p. A2.

Article in a Magazine

MLA   Mendelsohn, Daniel. "Deep Frieze: The Mystery of the Parthenon." *The New Yorker*, 14 Apr. 2014, pp. 34–39.

APA   Mendelsohn, D. (2014, April 14). Deep frieze: The mystery of the Parthenon. *The New Yorker, 90,* 34–39.

Anonymous Article in a Magazine

MLA   "The Myth of the Compassionate Execution." *Scientific American*, May 2014, p. 12.

APA   The myth of the compassionate execution. (2014, May). *Scientific American, 310,* 12.

Article in an Academic Journal

MLA   Brown, Bill. "The Origin of the American Work of Art." *American Literary History,* vol. 25, no. 4, 2013, pp. 772–802.

APA   Brown, B. (2013). The origin of the American work of art. *American Literary History 25(4),* 772–804.

Personal Interview

MLA   Gray, Richard. Personal interview. 10 Nov. 2016.

APA   In APA style, all personal communications (conversations, interviews, and the like) are excluded from the list of references. Such sources are documented only within the body of the text, like this:

Facilities & Operations Director R. Gray (personal communication, Nov. 10, 2016) stated that "the renovation project will take at least six weeks."

Link Within an Internet Site

MLA   "Healthy Work Environment." *Nursing World: American Nurses' Association,* www.nursingworld.org. Accessed 16 April 2017.

APA   Healthy Work Environment. *Nursing world: American Nurses' Association.* Retrieved April 16, 2017, from http://www.nursingworld.org.

Online Newspaper Article

MLA   Alford, Henry. "Feuding in 140 Characters." *The New York Times*, 25 April 2014. www.nytimes.com. Accessed 16 April 2017.

APA   Alford, H. (2014, April 25). Feuding in 140 characters. *The New York Times.* Retrieved April 16, 2017, from http://www.nytimes.com.

Online Magazine Article

MLA   Green, Emma. "The Origins of Office Speak." *The Atlantic*, 24 Apr. 2014. www.theatlantic.com. Accessed 16 April 2017.

APA   Green, E. (2014, April 24). The origins of office speak. *The Atlantic*. Retrieved April 16, 2017 from http://theatlantic.com.

Article in a Database

MLA   Boucher, Jill, et al. "Memory in Autistic Spectrum Disorder." *Psychological Bulletin*, vol. 138, no. 3, 2012, pp. 458–496. *ERIK*, Ebsco Host. 2 May 2015. Accessed 16 April 2017.

APA   Boucher, J., Mayes, A., & Bigham, S. (2012). Memory in autistic spectrum disorder. *Psychological Bulletin*, 138(3), 458–496. Retrieved April 16, 2017.

E-mail Message

MLA   Ahern, Edward. "Re: Vendor Contracts." Received by William Powers, 23 May 2017.

APA   In APA style, all personal communications (e-mail, conversations, interviews, and the like) are excluded from the list of references. Such sources are documented only within the text, like this:

Purchasing Director E. Ahern (personal communication, May 23, 2016) agreed that "all vendor contracts should be reviewed immediately."

The last several examples illustrate the basic formats recommended by the MLA and the APA for documenting electronic sources. As you can see, both styles provide essentially the same information that's used to identify print sources: the author's name (if known), the title of the work, and so on. Be aware, however, that although the new (eighth) edition of the *MLA Handbook* recommends the inclusion of URLs in your works-cited list (as in the relevant examples above), URLs are not always required: "if your instructor prefers that you not include them, follow his or her directions" (48). Further, electronic sources are of many different kinds, not all of which can be covered here. For a more complete explanation of how electronic (and print) sources are handled, you should consult the two organizations' websites or the most recent editions of their handbooks, readily available in virtually all academic libraries:

MLA Handbook. 8th ed. MLA, 2016.

Publication Manual of the American Psychological Association. 6th ed. APA, 2010.

In addition, there are numerous websites that actually provide you with bibliography entries in various styles, including MLA and APA. Typically, these sites employ a "fill in the blanks" approach. You type in the information and the computer does the rest. Of course, you must be very careful to enter the data correctly. The best of these sites can be found at www.easybib.com, although it charges a fee for styles other than MLA. Even more conveniently, Microsoft Word software includes a documentation feature that operates in much the same way and comprises MLA, APA, and other styles. In addition, many databases provide a "citation" option in the toolbar. However, the citation provided is not always in complete conformity with MLA or APA style, especially now that the MLA has introduced revised guidelines, which are detailed in the most recent edition of the *MLA Handbook*.

PARENTHETICAL CITATIONS

Every time you use a source within the body of a paper—whether summarizing, paraphrasing, or directly quoting—you must identify the source by inserting parentheses. The contents and positioning of these parentheses vary somewhat depending on whether you're using MLA or APA style. Here are examples of how to cite quotations:

MLA   "The Internet has enabled a flowering of easy-to-use publishing tools and given social media unprecedented reach and scale" (Standage 4).

APA   "The Internet has enabled a flowering of easy-to-use publishing tools and given social media unprecedented reach and scale" (Standage, 2013, pg. 4).

If you mention the author's name in your own text, neither MLA nor APA requires that the name appear in the parentheses, although the APA system then requires *two* parenthetical insertions. The first provides the date of publication and the second the page number.

MLA   As Standage observes, "The Internet has enabled a flowering of easy-to-use publishing tools and given social media unprecedented reach and scale" (4).

APA   As Standage (2013) observes, "The Internet has enabled a flowering of easy-to-use publishing tools and given social media unprecedented reach and scale" (p. 4).

When you're summarizing or paraphrasing, and whether mentioning the author's name or not, the differences between the two styles are as follows:

MLA   As Standage observes, the Internet's self-publishing tools have greatly expanded the scope of social media (4).

APA   As Standage (2013) observes, the Internet's self-publishing tools have greatly expanded the scope of social media (p. 4).

MLA   The Internet's self-publishing tools have greatly expanded the scope of social media (Standage 4).

APA   The Internet's self-publishing tools have greatly expanded the scope of social media (Standage, 2013, pg. 4).

To credit a quote from an unsigned source (such as the "Anonymous Article in a Magazine" example shown on pg. 190), do it as follows:

MLA   "Doctors and nurses are taught to first 'do no harm'; physicians are banned by professional ethics codes from participating in executions" ("The Myth" 12).

APA   "Doctors and nurses are taught to first 'do no harm'; physicians are banned by professional ethics codes from participating in executions" ("The myth," 2014, p. 12).

To credit a paraphrase from an unsigned source, follow the same pattern:

MLA   Both by training and ethical principles, health care professionals are prevented from performing executions ("The Myth" 12).

APA   Both by training and ethical principles, health care professionals are prevented from performing executions ("The myth," 2014, p. 12).

The purpose of parenthetical citations is to enable readers to find your sources on the "Works Cited" or "References" page in case they want to consult those sources in their entirety. Obviously, proper documentation is an important part of any paper that has drawn on sources beyond the writer's own prior knowledge. At the end of this chapter is a research-based essay in which the student has investigated the news events that took place on the day of her birth, and documented that paper using MLA guidelines.

CHECKLIST: RESEARCH-BASED ESSAY

A good research-based essay

▶ Has a meaningful title that clearly identifies the topic

▶ Opens with an interesting, attention-getting introduction that establishes the significance of the topic, and provides a firm thesis statement

▶ Is organized into several body paragraphs, enough to fully cover the topic, and proceeds in a coherent, step-by-step way, focusing on one main idea at a time

▶ Draws upon reliable sources of information

▶ Employs paraphrase, summary, and quotation correctly, avoiding plagiarism

▶ Closes with a smooth, meaningful conclusion that gracefully resolves the discussion by somehow relating back to the introduction

▶ Includes full documentation—bibliography and parenthetical citations—prepared in either MLA or APA format

▶ Uses clear, simple, straightforward language—nothing fancy

▶ Maintains an appropriate tone, neither too formal nor too conversational

▶ Contains no inappropriate material

▶ Contains no typos or mechanical errors in spelling, capitalization, punctuation, or grammar

▶ Satisfies the length requirements of the assignment

MODEL RESEARCH-BASED ESSAY

Nac 1

Sara Nac
Professor Rosemary Smith
English 101
December 11, 2017

News Events on My Birthday: November 10, 1995

I was born at St. Elizabeth's Hospital in Utica, New York, at 2:00 P.M. on Friday, November 10, 1995, weighing in at twelve pounds. My parents took me home to Edward Street, where they still reside today. This research-based essay will summarize some of the major news events that were reported in the media on the day of my birth, focusing on world, national, and local stories, along with sports and entertainment. I will also update each of the stories, placing them in contemporary perspective.

In world news, Ukraine and Macedonia ratified the European Convention on Human Rights, joining thirty-six other countries as members of the Council of Europe, an organization that "promotes democracy, monitors human rights and fosters cultural diversity" ("2 Nations" D1). Based in Strasbourg, France, the Council still exists today, and now has forty-seven member nations. ("47")

One highly controversial national story involved Jack Kevorkian, a Michigan physician who had become famous as "Dr. Death" for helping terminally ill people commit suicide. He was charged with the murder of Patricia Cashman, 58, of San Marcos, California, after helping her inhale lethal exhaust fumes from her car ("After" A20). She was the twenty-sixth person known to have sought his assistance since 1990 (Borg). Kevorkian was acquitted, as he had been many times before, but was finally convicted in 1999 after participating in yet another voluntary suicide, that of Thomas Youk, 51, of Detroit, and was sentenced to ten to twenty-five years in prison ("Kevorkian Case"). In 2007, however, he was released after earning "time off for good behavior" ("Kevorkian Released"). An HBO movie about him, *You Don't Know Jack*, starring Al Pacino, was released in 2010 ("You"). He died in 2011 at age 83. (Schneider A1)

On the local scene, Democrat Ed Hanna, who had been Utica's mayor from 1974 to 1977, returned to that office by winning a close three-way race, defeating four-term incumbent Republican Louis LaPolla and Independent Barbara Klein (Crockett 1A). Four years later he was reelected, getting 75% of the vote, but resigned in 2000 because of health issues and was replaced by common council president Tim Julian, who remained in office until 2007. Hanna ran against Julian in 2007, but both lost to David Roefaro (Dufresne). Hanna died in 2009 at the age of 86. As Julian said, "His methods were sometimes unconventional, but he had a certain knack of getting the people to rally behind him" ("Hanna"). Today Utica's mayor is Robert Palmieri.

In sports, the Chicago Bulls remained undefeated, winning their fourth straight basketball game, a 106-88 drubbing of the Cleveland Cavaliers. As usual, the Bulls' high-scorer was All-Star Michael Jordan, with 29 points. But Jordan's teammate Scottie Pippen also sparkled, recording a rare triple-double, with 18 points, 13 rebounds, and 12 assists ("Triple-Double" B14). The Bulls were the most dominant NBA team of the 1990s, winning six championships as Jordan established himself as one of the very greatest players of all time ("History"). Jordan and Pippen are now retired, and both are in the Basketball Hall of Fame. ("Hall")

Among the Hollywood movies in the theaters on my birthday was *The American President*, a "comedy-drama about a widowed United States president and a lobbyist who fall in love." Michael Douglas plays the president and Annette Bening the lobbyist. Directed by Rob Reiner, the movie was rated PG-13 ("The American"). Douglas, one of America's most celebrated actors, has starred in a great many other films. Bening has also won many awards, including The Screen Actors Guild "Best Female Actress in a Leading Role" recognition for her performance in *American Beauty*. ("Annette")

So there you have it: a selection of some of the highlights of my birthday twenty-two years ago. To my parents, however, probably none of these occurrences seemed very important, as they were undoubtedly more focused on my arrival!

Works Cited

"After Kevorkian-Aided Suicide, Clash Over How Ill Woman Was." *The New York Times*, 10 Nov. 1995, p. A20. *ProQuest Historical Newspapers: The New York Times with Index.* Accessed 20 Nov. 2017.

"The American President." *IMNb: The Internet Movie Database.* www.imdb.com. Accessed 20 Nov. 2017.

"Annette Bening." *Moviefone.* www.moviefone.com. Accessed 20 Nov. 2017.

Borg, Gary. "Kevorkian Uses His 'Machine' To Assist in Latest Aided Suicide." *Chicago Tribune*, 13 Nov. 1995. www.chicagotribune.org. Accessed 20 Nov. 2017.

Crockett, Alan D. "It's Hanna: Vote Recount Makes Him Utica Mayor, Again." *Observer-Dispatch*, 10 Nov. 1995. www.uticaod.com. Accessed 20 Nov. 2017.

Dufresne, Debbie. "Timeline of the Life and Career of Edward A. Hanna." *Observer-Dispatch*, 14 Mar. 2009. wwwuticaod.com. Accessed 20 Nov. 2017.

"47 Member States." *Council of Europe.* www.coe.int. Accessed 20 Nov. 2017.

"Hall of Famers." *Naismith Memorial Basketball Hall of Fame.* www.hoophall.com. Accessed 20 Nov. 2017.

"Hanna Dead at 86; Funeral Arrangements Set." *Observer-Dispatch,* 13 Mar. 2009. www.uticaod.com. Accessed 20 Nov. 2017.

"History of the Chicago Bulls." *The Official Site of the Chicago Bulls.* www.bulls.com. Accessed 20 Nov. 2017.

"Kervorkian Case: Kevorkian Sentenced to 10 to 25 Years." *CNN,* 31 Dec. 2007. www.cnn.org. Accessed 20 Nov. 2017.

"Kevorkian Released After 8 Years: Suicide Activist Says He Will Obey the Law but Try to Change It." *Washington Post,* 2 June 2007. www.washingtonpost.com. Accessed 20 Nov. 2017.

Schneider, Keith. "Jack Kevorkian, 1928-2011: Doctor Who Helped End Lives." *The New York Times*, 4 June 2011, p. A1. *ProQuest Historical Newspapers: The New York Times with Index.* Accessed 20 Nov. 2017.

"Triple-Double for Pippen." *The New York Times*, 10 Nov. 1995, p. B14. *ProQuest Historical Newspapers: The New York Times with Index.* Accessed 20 Nov. 2017.

"2 Nations Join Panel for Rights in Europe." *The New York Times*, 10 Nov. 1995, p. A12. *ProQuest Historical Newspapers: The New York Times with Index.* Accessed 20 Nov. 2017.

"You Don't Know Jack." *HBO Movies.* www.hbo.com. Accessed 20 Nov. 2017.

EXERCISES

1. Revise the "Works Cited" page of Sara Nac's "birthday" paper, using APA style.

2. Revise the parenthetical citations in that paper, using APA style.

3. Exercise 1 in Chapter 16 required you to find five sources of information on the topic of cigarette smoking among doctors and nurses. Now prepare an MLA-style "Works Cited" page and an APA-style "References" page listing those sources:

   ▶ a chapter in an edited book
   ▶ an article in a popular magazine
   ▶ an article in a medical journal
   ▶ an article in a major newspaper
   ▶ a discussion on a website

APPENDICES

Seven Style Tips

CREATE ACTIVE SENTENCES WITH SUBJECTS AND VERBS SIDE BY SIDE

In an active sentence, the subject is the actor, performing the action of the verb. In a passive sentence, the subject is not the actor, and in fact *receives* the action of the verb.

	(Subject/Actor)	(Verb/Action)	
ACTIVE:	The cat	chased	the rat.

	(Subject/Receiver)	(Verb/Action)	
PASSIVE:	The rat	was chased	by the cat.

Because the active approach requires fewer words, it's usually preferable. Of course, there are situations in which you may choose to use the passive approach—for emphasis or variety, perhaps. Or you may want to "hide" the actor, when writing about a situation in which some mistake or controversial decision has been made. Here's an example:

	(Subject/Actor)	(Verb/Action)	
ACTIVE:	Linda Fraser	decided	that the class should complain to the Dean.

	(Subject/Receiver)	(Verb/Action)	
PASSIVE:	A decision	was made	that the class should complain to the Dean.

Obviously, the passive would probably be better in a case like this. There is no reason to bring Linda Fraser's identity to the attention of anyone who may later wish to retaliate against her. But use the passive only with good cause; every use of the passive should be purposefully deliberate rather than accidental.

The heart of any sentence, whether active or passive, is the main verb and its subject. Therefore, English sentences are easiest to understand when subjects and verbs are as close together as possible. For example, both of the following sentences are grammatical, but the second is smoother because the first creates an interruption between the main subject and verb.

(Subject)   (Verb)

Food servers, because kitchen doors always open to the right, should learn to carry trays left-handed.

(Subject)   (Verb)

Because kitchen doors always open to the right, food servers should learn to carry trays left-handed.

Whenever possible, try to keep subjects and verbs side by side. This will not only ensure maximum clarity, but will also help you avoid grammatical errors involving subject/verb agreement. (See Appendix B, page 218.)

POSITION MODIFIERS NEAR WHAT THEY MODIFY

A modifier is a word or phrase that makes another word or phrase more specific by limiting or qualifying its sense. For example, in the phrase *my English book*, the words *my* and *English* modify the word *book*. In the sentence, *Exhausted, he fell asleep at the wheel*, the word *Exhausted* modifies the word *he*, the word *asleep* modifies the word *fell*, and the phrase *at the wheel* modifies the word *asleep*. That sentence is easy to understand partly because all the modifiers are where they belong. But consider this rather different example:

Growing in the garden, Lisa's mother found marijuana.

Certainly Lisa's mother was not growing in the garden. But that's what the sentence says, because the modifying phrase *growing in the garden* is misplaced, "dangling" off the front of the sentence. Really it should be alongside what it modifies (*marijuana*), like this:

Lisa's mother found marijuana growing in the garden.

Of course, nobody would be likely to misinterpret the original version of that sentence, but misplaced modifiers can indeed create confusion when more than one interpretation is possible. Just as subjects and verbs work best when side-by-side, modifiers should always be positioned as close as possible to what they modify.

NOTE: The modifier *only* is nearly always misplaced, as in this sentence:

I only have two dollars.

Certainly the sentence should be revised as follows, because *only* modifies *two*, not *have*:

I have only two dollars.

USE TRANSITIONS EFFECTIVELY

Transitional words or phrases serve as links between sentence parts, whole sentences, or paragraphs, clarifying the relationships among ideas. In effect, they serve as "bridges" from idea to idea within a piece of writing and are therefore quite helpful to the reader. In general, longer transitions—words such as *therefore* and *consequently* and clusters of words like *on the other hand* or *in conclusion*—tend to appear at the beginning of a sentence, followed by a comma, while short transitions—like *and, but,* and *so*—tend to appear within sentences, often with a comma before them. Transitions can be loosely categorized according to the kinds of relationships they signal. This chart will help you choose a correct transition in each situation.

Signal	Transition
Additional Information	and, also, furthermore, in addition, moreover
Example	for example, for instance, to illustrate
Explanation	in other words, simply stated, that is
Similarity	in like manner, likewise, similarly
Contrast	but, yet, conversely, however, nevertheless, on the other hand
Cause and Effect	accordingly, as a result, because, consequently, hence, so, therefore, thus
Emphasis	clearly, indeed, in fact, obviously
Summary	finally, in conclusion, in short, to sum up

HANDLE NUMBERS CORRECTLY

Frequently we must decide whether to spell out a number or use a numeral (for example, *three hundred* or *300*). This issue is somewhat complicated, because several different systems exist. Usually, however, words are used for amounts from zero to nine, and sometimes for other amounts that can be expressed in one or two words, such as thirty-one or fifty. (Note that two-word numbers under 100 require a hyphen.)

Here are a few guidelines that may help:

▶ Never begin a sentence with a numeral. Either spell it out or, if the number is large, reorder the sentence so the numeral appears elsewhere.

ORIGINAL: 781 students have bought concert tickets so far.

REVISION: So far, 781 students have bought concert tickets.

▶ For very large numbers, combine numerals and words, as in "100 million."

▶ Combine numerals and words whenever such an approach will prevent misreading, as in this example:

ORIGINAL: You will need 3 6 inch screws and 10 4 inch nails.

REVISION: You will need three 6-inch screws and ten 4-inch nails.

Note that a hyphen is required when a number is used with a word to modify another word.

▶ Be consistent about how you deal with numbers in a given piece of writing. Pick one approach and stick with it, as in this example:

ORIGINAL: She took five courses in the spring and 2 in the summer.

REVISION: She took five courses in the spring and two in the summer.

► Use numerals for all statistical data, such as the following:

ages and addresses

dates

exact amounts of money

fractions and decimals

identification numbers

measurements (including height and weight)

page numbers

percentages, ratios, proportions

scores

When dealing with statistics, it often makes sense to combine numerals with other symbols rather than with words (*e.g.*, 6′1″ rather than 6 feet, 1 inch and $375 rather than 375 dollars).

USE FAMILIAR VOCABULARY—NOTHING FANCY

Most readers do not respond well to fancy wording. Therefore, you should use ordinary terms your reader will immediately recognize and understand. This is true even when your reader is your professor, who is almost certainly well-educated and equipped with a larger than average vocabulary. Your professor will *understand* inflated diction, but will probably regard it as an irritating (because transparent) attempt to hide weak content beneath the camouflage of ornate language. Keep it simple.

Of course, there's no reason to avoid *technical* terms—specialized words for which there are no satisfactory substitutes—if your reader can be expected to know them. An electrode is an electrode, a condenser is a condenser, and an isometric drawing is an isometric drawing. If you're writing in a technical context, most of your readers (and certainly your professor) will share your knowledge of the subject area. If you're not sure whether your reader is familiar with the vocabulary of the field, provide a glossary (a list of words with their definitions) somewhere within the document. If there are only a few potentially troublesome terms, you can insert parenthesized definitions—as in the previous sentence, where *glossary* is defined.

Generally, however, the best policy is to use the simplest word available, provided it's accurate: *Pay* rather than *remunerate; transparent* rather than *pellucid; steal* rather than *pilfer*. Another advantage of using everyday language is that your spelling will improve, especially when handwriting without the benefit of an electronic spell-checker. You're far more likely to misspell words you're unaccustomed to seeing in print, because you won't know whether they "look right" on the page.

WRITE SHORT SENTENCES

A sentence can be very long and still be grammatical. Many highly-regarded writers—the prize-winning American novelist William Faulkner, for example—have favored highly elaborate sentence structure. But most of us are not trying to become the next Faulkner. We write for a different purpose—usually to convey information, rather than to dazzle or impress. And the longer a sentence becomes, the harder it is for the reader to process. If a sentence goes much beyond twenty-five or thirty words, the reader's comprehension decreases.

To ensure maximum readability, therefore, limit your sentence length to an *average* of no more than twenty words. This can be inhibiting during the actual composing process, so make such adjustments afterwards, when revising.

It's usually fairly easy to see where the breaks should be (after each main idea), as in this example:

ORIGINAL

Athletes who gripe during practice or play practical jokes in the locker room may think they're relieving tension on the team, but in fact they may only be contributing to it, because a really good team is composed of players who rarely argue, seldom complain, and never criticize one another, understanding that a good team is like any efficient organization, in which every individual has a specific role to play, so players should submerge their individual egos for the sake of fostering team unity.

(One 83-word sentence)

REVISION

Athletes who gripe during practice or play practical jokes in the locker room may think they're relieving tension on the team. But in fact they may only be contributing to it. A really good team is composed of players who rarely argue, seldom complain, and never criticize one another. They understand that a good team is like any efficient organization, in which every individual has a specific role. Players should submerge their individual egos for the sake of fostering team unity.

(Five sentences, 16-word average)

Judging whether a sentence is too long, however, depends on context: What comes before it and what comes after. An occasional long sentence is acceptable, especially before or after a short one.

EDIT FOR CONCISION AND ECONOMY

Although everything already discussed in this chapter is crucial to developing a clear, easily readable style, the most important principle of all is to avoid wordiness and strive for concision and economy. Good writing is simple and direct. Of course, achieving a plainspoken, reader-friendly style is far easier said than done. But it becomes somewhat easier if you learn to recognize the five main sources of verbal clutter.

Unnecessary Introductions

Practically all writers waste words, especially in a first draft. But excess verbiage interferes with communication by inflating sentence length and tiring the reader. The unnecessary introduction, for example, is among the most common kinds of verbal clutter.

It's perfectly acceptable—and sometimes necessary—to open a sentence with an introductory phrase that leads into the main idea. But this depends on who the reader is, what the circumstances are, and other factors. Check your writing for *needless* introductions—phrases in which you're simply "clearing your throat," as in these examples:

As I look back on what I have said in this essay, it seems that...

Though this might not seem very important, you should remember that...

Because all of us attended last Friday's lecture, there is no need to summarize that presentation, in which the speaker said that...

Instead, get right to the point:

> It seems that…
>
> You should remember that…
>
> In last Friday's lecture, the speaker said that…

Submerged Verbs

Like unnecessary introductions, submerged verbs are a major source of verbal clutter. Too often we use a verb plus another verb (hidden or "submerged" within a noun) when one verb (the submerged one) would do, as in phrases like the following:

> (Verb)   (Noun)   (Verb)
> Come to a conclusion = conclude
>
> (Verb) (Noun)   (Verb)
> reach a decision = decide
>
> (Verb) (Noun)   (Verb)
> give a summary = summarize

Instead, simply use the "submerged" verb: *Conclude, decide,* and *summarize.* This approach is far better because it reduces sentence length by expressing ideas more directly.

Self-Evident Modifiers

Sometimes we use words quite unnecessarily, expressing already self-evident ideas, as in these redundant modifiers:

> (Modifier)
> my personal opinion   *All* opinions are "personal."
>
> (Modifier)
> Visible to the eye   Anything visible *must be* visible "to the eye."
>
> (Modifier)
> Past history   *All* history is "past."

In each case, it would be better to omit the modifier and use a single word: *Opinion, visible,* and *history.*
  The American Psychological Association (APA) *Publication Manual* includes more than a dozen excellent examples of redundancy, including the following. In each, the underlining identifies unnecessary words.

they were both alike	one and the same
a total of 68 participants	in close proximity
four different groups	completely unanimous
exactly the same	just the same
absolutely essential	small in size

Long-Winded Expressions

As we have seen, unnecessary introductions and submerged verbs create bothersome clutter, but any long-winded expression using more words than necessary wastes the reader's time and energy. Here are ten familiar examples:

ORIGINAL	REVISION
at this point in time	now
despite the fact that	although
due to the fact that	because
during the time that	while
in many instances	often
in order to	to
in the course of	during
in the event that	if
in the near future	soon
on two occasions	twice

A great many common clichés also fall into this category. Try to cultivate the habit of boiling down several words into one whenever possible.

Repetitious Wording

As we've seen, several short sentences are usually preferable to one long one. But sometimes it's better to combine two or three short sentences to avoid unnecessarily repeating ourselves. If this is done correctly, the resulting sentence is significantly shorter than the total length of the several sentences that went into it, as in this example:

ORIGINAL

The electric drill is easier to use than the hand drill. The electric drill is faster than the hand drill. The electric drill is a very useful tool. (28 words)

REVISION

Easier and faster to use than the hand drill, the electric drill is a very useful tool. (17 words)

In the original, "the electric drill" appears three times and "the hand drill" twice. By using each of these phrases only once, the revision conveys the same information much more efficiently. Always strive for this level of economy.

Review of Mechanics: Spelling, Punctuation, and Grammar

SPELLING

Most of us experience at least some difficulty with spelling. You can become a better speller, however, simply by observing the following basic guidelines:

1. Do not concern yourself with spelling while you're composing. Concentrate on content, clarity, and organization instead. But at the rewriting stage, carefully check for obvious errors—words you know how to spell but got wrong through carelessness. Do not permit such blunders to slip past you. When in doubt, consult the dictionary. And correct the words highlighted by your computer's spell-checker. But understand that electronic aids are not foolproof. Although quite helpful in spotting typos, spelling checkers are no substitute for vigilance on the part of the writer.

2. Certain pairs of homonyms—words that sound alike but are spelled differently—give nearly everyone trouble, especially since electronic spell-checkers will not catch the error if you pick the wrong homonym. Memorize this list of commonly confused words:

   accept: to receive willingly
   except: with the exception of

   He cannot **accept** criticism.
   I like everyone **except** Roger.

   affect: to produce an effect upon
   effect: that which is produced, a result

   Humidity will always **affect** you.
   That film had an **effect** upon me.

   alot: [no such word]
   a lot: a great many

   A lot of people fear snakes.

   a while: for a period of time
   awhile: *for* a while

   He studied for **a while.**
   He studied **awhile.**

   cite: to quote or mention
   site: a physical location
   sight: something seen

   Always **cite** your sources.
   The job **site** is on Route 12.
   It was a **sight** to behold!

   its: possessive form of *it*
   it's: contraction (*it is*)

   The cat ate **its** food.
   It's raining hard today.

loose: not tight	He prefers **loose** clothing.
lose: to misplace	I hate to **lose** my keys.
passed: past tense of *to pass*	She **passed** the test with a 98%.
past: gone by in time	Try not to repeat **past** mistakes.
their: possessive form of *they*	**Their** car
there: in or at that place	is over **there**,
they're: contraction (*they are*)	but **they're** over here.
to: expresses movement toward	We've sent astronauts **to** the moon.
too: also, more than enough	Me **too**! **Too** much crime.
two: 2	She has **two** brothers.
whose: possessive form of *who*	**Whose** hat is this?
who's: contraction (*who is* or *who has*)	**Who's** going to the movie tonight?
	Who's already seen this movie?
your: possessive form of *you*	**Your** mother always praises you
you're: contraction (*you are*)	because **you're** a good son.

3. We all have certain words we nearly always misspell, a handful of terms we repeatedly get wrong. Identify your own "problem" words, make a list of them, and consult it whenever you must use one of these words. Eventually you'll no longer need the list as the correct spellings imprint themselves on your memory.

4. As mentioned in Appendix A, pg. 204, you should avoid fancy words you're unaccustomed to seeing in print. Use ordinary, everyday vocabulary instead. Not only will your reader understand more easily, but you'll be more likely to notice if anything "looks wrong" because of misspelling.

5. For the spelling of specialized or technical terms, check manuals and the indexes of textbooks in your field of study.

6. Memorize some basic rules. English spelling is highly inconsistent and filled with exceptions, but there are some generally reliable patterns:

   ▶ *i* before *e*, as in

      achieve, belief, cashier
      except after *c*, as in
      conceit, deceive, receipt

   Notice that in all the above examples, the two letters *i* and *e* combine to sound like a long *e*. If they combine to sound like anything else, the "*i* before *e* except after *c*" rule no longer applies, as in

      height [long *i* sound] and **weight** [long *a* sound]

   ▶ When adding a suffix (an ending) to a word that ends in *e*, keep the *e* if the suffix begins with a consonant, as in

      arrange, arrangement
      extreme, extremely
      hope, hopeless

Drop the *e* if the suffix begins with a vowel, as in

advertise, advertising
debate, debated
elevate, elevation

▶ When adding a suffix to a word that ends in a consonant followed by *y*, change the *y* to *i* unless the suffix begins with *i*, as in

angry, angrier
funny, funniest
worry, worried

▶ When adding a suffix to a word that ends in a consonant, double the consonant only if

the consonant is preceded by a vowel;
the word is one syllable, or accented on the last syllable;
the suffix begins with a vowel, as in

cram, crammed
scan, scanning
spam, spammed

▶ When choosing between the suffixes *–able* and *–ible*, remember that most of the *–able* words are "able" to stand alone without the suffix, as in **affordable** and **remarkable**, while most of the *–ible* words cannot, such as **eligible** and **legible**.

▶ To make a word plural, add *–es* if the pluralizing creates an additional syllable, unless the word already ends in *-e*; otherwise just add an *–s*.

1 class, 2 classes
1 house, 2 houses
1 section, 2 sections

But if the word ends in a consonant followed by *o*, add *–es* even if the pluralizing does not create an extra syllable

1 hero, 2 heroes
1 motto, 2 mottoes

Remember that some words are made plural by changes *within* those words.

1 goose, 2 geese
1 man, 2 men
1 mouse, 2 mice

And some words are the same in both the singular and the plural.

1 deer, 2 deer
1 fish, 2 fish

Lastly, remember <u>never</u> to pluralize a word by using an apostrophe. The apostrophe is used only in contractions and to indicate possession. (See Appendix B, pg. 216.)

PUNCTUATION

Punctuation exists not to make writers' lives more difficult but to make readers' lives easier. A punctuation mark is simply a symbol, like a road sign on a highway. It tells readers when to slow down, when to stop, and how to anticipate and respond to what appears before them on the page. This brings us to a basic principle: Trust your ear; listen to the sentence and insert punctuation marks wherever you can hear them.

Be careful not to punctuate excessively. As on a highway, an incorrect sign is even more misleading than a missing one. Consider this sentence, for example:

> Shakespeare is revered, of course, as a playwright, but he also authored some of the most outstanding sonnets in the English language.

No real harm would result if those commas were removed, because the reader would probably pause at the appropriate points instinctively and the missing commas would in no way obscure the meaning. But look at this version:

> Shakespeare, is revered, of course, as a, playwright, but, he also authored, some, of the most, outstanding, sonnets, in the English, language.

See how much harder it is to read the sentence? All those unnecessary commas cause the reader to hesitate repeatedly, thereby derailing the train of thought. And the reader *will* keep pausing, because we automatically respond to symbols whether we want to or not. Admittedly, few writers would over-punctuate the sentence to that degree, but a second basic principle emerges: *Do not punctuate at all unless you're pretty sure you should; when in doubt, leave it out.*

Of course, there's more to punctuation than these two principles. As you know, there are hundreds of punctuation rules. But the good news is that—unless you plan to become a professional writer or editor—you need to know only a small percentage of them. This section of the Appendix covers the basics everyone must know to punctuate adequately.

End Punctuation: Period, Question Mark, and Exclamation Mark

Practically everyone knows how to use periods, question marks, and exclamation marks at the ends of sentences. Sometimes, however, we simply forget to insert end punctuation because the mind is faster than the hand. As we write, we tend to think ahead a sentence or two, and it's easy to overlook end punctuation in our rush to express the next thought. This is something to watch for at the rewriting stage. Make sure that every sentence ends with punctuation. Be especially vigilant about question marks. A common error is to hastily insert a period even though the sentence is actually a question. As for exclamation marks, use them rarely. If used too often, they lose their impact, much like "four letter words" in conversation. Use exclamation marks only when necessary to signal emphasis.

Comma

The comma is probably the most difficult of all punctuation marks to use correctly because it's required in such a wide range of situations. But if you study the following rules you'll notice that it's also the easiest punctuation mark to "hear." As mentioned earlier, trust your ear in determining where to insert commas. And when in doubt, leave it out. The following guidelines will help:

▶ Use commas to separate words or phrases in a sequence, as in these examples:

> There are five teams in the American League East: Baltimore, Boston, New York, Tampa Bay, and Toronto.

The mayor met with the city council, reassuring them about the budget crisis, addressing their fears about escalating crime, and promising to investigate recent school board controversies.

Notice that there's a comma before the *and* in both of these sentences. Sometimes called "the Oxford comma," it's optional in sequences of nouns (as in the first example), but is required in sequences of *phrases* (as in the second example). Play it safe: Always use it.

▶ Use a comma after an introductory word or phrase, as in these examples:

Obviously, everyone should quit smoking.

Despite the team's best efforts, we lost the basketball game by two points.

▶ Use commas before "linking" words such as *and, but,* or *so* if the word is linking two complete sentences, as in these examples:

Appetizers usually appear at the beginning of a menu, and desserts usually appear at the end.

The risks involved in mountain climbing are many, but so are the rewards.

Most high-performance cars do not get good gas mileage, so they are expensive to take on long trips.

▶ Use commas between two or more adjectives in a row, but only if those adjectives would make sense in any order, as in this example:

Solving a difficult mathematical equation can be a long, slow process.

In the following example, there are no commas between the adjectives (*three, more,* and *full*) because they make sense only in the order given:

The senator served three more full terms in office.

▶ Use commas to surround words or phrases that are not essential to the sense of the sentence—words or phrases that could just as easily appear in parentheses, as in these examples:

Bananas, which are rich in potassium, are a healthy snack food.

James Joyce, the famous Irish novelist, was a very influential writer.

La Sagrada Familia, a basilica located in Barcelona, is an amazing architectural achievement.

▶ Use a comma before an afterthought—a word or phrase "tacked on" at the end of a sentence—as in these examples:

Global warming is a major problem, despite some misinformed people's refusal to take it seriously.

Self-help books are very popular, although most have little new to say.

The first hockey goalie to wear a protective mask was Jacques Plante, who starred for Montreal in the 1950s.

▶ Use a comma before a direct quote, as in these examples:

> Nathan Hale said, "I only regret that I have but one life to give for my country."
>
> The professor asked, "How many people have finished the assignment?"
>
> What famous writer said, "The reports of my death have been greatly exaggerated"?

Colon and Semicolon

The colon and the semicolon are obviously related, but they serve different purposes and should not be used interchangeably.

The three main uses of the colon are after the salutation of a business letter, to introduce a complicated list, and to introduce a long quote, as in these examples:

> There are several advantages to operating a franchise such as McDonald's or Arby's rather than attempting to open your own business: management training and assistance; a recognized name, product, and operating concept; and financial assistance during start-up.

> All Boy Scouts are required to learn the Scout Oath: "On my honor I will do my best to do my duty to God and my country and to obey the Scout Law; to help other people at all times; to keep myself physically strong, mentally awake and morally straight."

Other uses of the colon are in denoting time of day (3:05 a.m.) and "stopwatch" time (1:07:31), in Biblical citations (Corinthians 3:22), in two-part book and article titles (*A Woman in Charge: The Life of Hillary Rodham Clinton*), and in various locations within bibliography entries (see Chapter 17). It can also be used to serve a "stop/go" function, as in *Some coaches care about only one thing: winning.*

▶ There are really only two uses for the semicolon: to link two complete sentences that are closely related, and to separate the items in a complicated list, as in the *franchise* and *Scout Oath* examples above. The semicolon should generally be avoided, however, because there's usually a better alternative. When linking closely related sentences, for example, a comma along with a transition word like *and*, *but*, or *so* will not only establish the connection but also clarify the relationship between the ideas. Compare these examples:

> She didn't study; she failed the test.
>
> She didn't study, so she failed the test.

Clearly, the second version is better. It not only connects the two sentences but plainly shows that the second fact is the result of the first.

As for separating the items in a complicated list, simply arrange the items vertically, perhaps with bullets, like this:

There are several advantages to operating a franchise such as McDonald's or Arby's rather than attempting to open your own business:

- ▶ management training and assistance
- ▶ a recognized name, product, and operating concept
- ▶ financial assistance during start-up

Again, the second version is obviously preferable. It enables the reader to differentiate more easily among the separate items.

Quotation Marks

Quotation marks are used to surround the title of a short work (e.g., a newspaper or magazine article, a story, or a poem), a direct quotation (someone else's exact words) or to show that a word or phrase is being used sarcastically, ironically, or in some other non-literal way. Here are examples:

TITLE:	Thomas Paine wrote "Common Sense."
DIRECT QUOTE:	The Nike motto is, "Just do it."
NONLITERAL USE:	No student wants to "bomb" on an exam.

Quotation marks must be positioned correctly in relation to other punctuation, especially end punctuation. Follow these guidelines:

- A period at the end of a sentence always goes inside the quotation marks.

  A well-known proverb is, "There's no free lunch."

- A question mark at the end of a sentence goes inside the quotation marks if the quote itself is a question.

  Juliet cries, "Wherefore art thou Romeo?"

- A question mark at the end of a sentence goes outside the quotation marks if the whole sentence (rather than the quote) is a question. Notice that in such a situation there is no period within the final quotation mark.

  Have you ever heard the proverb, "There's no free lunch"?

- A question mark at the end of a sentence goes inside the quotation marks if the quote and the whole sentence are both questions.

  Does Juliet cry, "Wherefore art thou Romeo?"

- If an attributing phrase (or anything else) follows the quote, the comma goes inside the quotation marks.

  "There's no free lunch," said my uncle.

- If an attributing phrase follows a quote that is a question, omit the comma but leave the question mark inside the quotation marks.

  "Wherefore art thou Romeo?" cries Juliet.

- For exclamation marks, simply follow the same pattern as for question marks.

Paul yelled, "No way!"	(Quote is emphatic.)
Don't you dare say, "Maybe"!	(Sentence is emphatic, quote is not.)
Don't you dare yell, "No way!"	(Quote and sentence are both emphatic.)
"No way!" yelled Paul.	(Emphatic quote is followed by attribution.)

Apostrophe

The apostrophe is often misused, partly because it can't be heard, but the rules governing this punctuation mark are actually quite simple.

1. *Never* use the apostrophe to make a word plural.

    INCORRECT: College student's must master many subject's.

    CORRECT: College students must master many subjects.

2. Use the apostrophe to make a word possessive, as follows:

    ▶ If the word is singular, add *'s*

        one child's hat
        one man's hat
        one woman's hat
        John Jones's hat
        Jane Smith's hat

    ▶ If the word is plural and does not already end in *–s*, add *'s*

        the children's hats
        the men's hats
        the women's hats

    ▶ If the word is plural and ends in *–s*, add an apostrophe

        the boys' hats
        the girls' hats
        the Joneses' house
        the Smiths' house

3. Use an apostrophe to replace the missing letter(s) in a contraction.

    I am, I'm   I will, I'll
    should have, should've   could have, could've
    should not, shouldn't   could not, couldn't
    would have, would've   do not, don't
    would not, wouldn't   does not, doesn't
    she is, she's   has not, hasn't
    is not, isn't   will not, won't

GRAMMAR

As with spelling and punctuation, there are a great many grammar rules. For practical purposes, however, you really need to know relatively few. This section focuses only on the basics—the rules governing sentence fragments, run-ons, and agreement.

Sentence Fragments

As the term itself denotes, a sentence fragment is an incomplete sentence. Most fragments are actually the result of faulty punctuation—when a writer inserts end punctuation too soon, thereby "stranding" part of the sentence. Consider these examples:

Rabies has been a problem since the 1950s throughout New York State.

(Fragment)
<u>Including Long Island and New York City</u>.

[The first period should have been a comma.]

(Fragment)
<u>If you fail to cite your sources in your research paper.</u> You are guilty of plagiarizing.

[Again, the first period should have been a comma.]

You can usually avoid sentence fragments if you remember three basic rules:

1. To be complete, a sentence must include a subject (actor) and a verb (action).

    (Subject)   (Verb)
    <u>Snowmobilers</u> sometimes <u>take</u> unnecessary risks.

2. If a sentence begins with a word or phrase that seems to point toward a two-part idea (for example, "if this, then that"), the second part must be included within the sentence, because the first part is a fragment and therefore cannot stand alone. For an example, see the "**If** you fail to cite" sentence above. Here are some other words that signal a two-part idea:

after	although	because
before	for	since
unless	until	when

3. Certain verb forms (some *-ed* forms, *-ing* forms, and *to* forms) cannot serve as the main verb in a sentence unless their subjects are expressed.

    (Fragment)
    <u>Opened in 1939.</u> The Merritt Parkway in Connecticut was one of America's first freeways.

    (Fragment)
    <u>Winding from Chicago to Los Angeles.</u> Route 66 covers 42,000 miles.

    (Fragment)
    <u>To succeed in your own business.</u> You need both energy and luck.

Notice that the *-ed, -ing,* and *to* forms frequently appear in introductory phrases. Learn to recognize these for what they are—not sentences in themselves but *beginnings* of sentences—and punctuate each with a comma, not a period. (See the second rule in the section on commas.)

Run-On Sentences

While the sentence fragment is something to avoid, even worse is a sentence that goes on and on after it should've stopped. A run-on sentence spills over into the following sentence with no break in between. When that happens, the writing takes on a rushed, headlong quality, and ideas become jumbled together.

There are two ways that a sentence can overflow into the next: either with a comma weakly separating the two sentences or with nothing at all in between. Here's an example of each:

A surveyor's measurements must be precise, there is no room for error.

A surveyor's measurements must be precise there is no room for error.

Technically, only the second example is a true run-on. The first is really an instance of what grammarians call a comma splice. For practical purposes, however, the problem is the same. In both cases, the first sentence has collided with the second. Obviously, the two sentences must be separated.

A surveyor's measurements must be precise. There is no room for error.

Another option would be to use a linking word to join the two sentences, thereby clarifying the relationship between them.

A surveyor's measurements must be precise, because there is no room for error.

Or you may prefer to turn one of the sentences into a fragment and use it as an introductory construction.

Because there is no room for error, a surveyor's measurements must be precise.

It should be clear by now that fragments and run-ons alike are usually the result of faulty punctuation. Certain patterns are correct, while others are not, as the following list indicates:

Correct Patterns	**Incorrect Patterns**
Sentence.	Fragment.
Sentence. Sentence.	Fragment. Fragment.
Sentence, link + sentence.	Sentence, sentence.
Fragment, sentence.	Fragment. Sentence.
Sentence, fragment.	Sentence. Fragment.
Fragment, sentence, fragment.	Fragment. Sentence. Fragment.

Subject-Verb Agreement

Another common grammar error is to use a plural verb with a singular subject, or vice versa. Remember that a singular subject requires a singular verb, while a plural subject requires a plural verb.

(Singular Subject)	(Singular Verb)	(Plural Subject)	(Plural Verb)
A singer	sings.	Singers	sing.

Note that singular subjects rarely end in *-s*, while singular verbs usually do. Conversely, plural subjects usually do end in *-s*, but plural verbs never do.

Although the subject-verb agreement rules may seem obvious, many writers commit agreement errors simply because they fail to distinguish between singular and plural subjects. This sometimes occurs when the subject is an indefinite pronoun, most of which are singular. Here's a chart of the most common such pronouns, indicating which ones are singular, which plural, and which can function as either:

Singular			Plural	Either
anybody	everybody	no one	few	all
anyone	everyone	nothing	many	any
anything	everything	somebody	several	more
each	neither	someone		most
either	nobody	something		none
				some

Agreement errors can also result when there's a cluster of words between the subject and its verb, thereby creating a misleading sound pattern.

INCORRECT   A pile of tools **are** on the workbench.
CORRECT   A pile of tools **is** on the workbench.

Even though *tools are* sounds correct, the first sentence is incorrect because *pile*—not *tools*—is the (singular) subject, and therefore requires the singular verb *is*.

Pronoun-Antecedent Agreement

Just as subjects and verbs must agree, so too must pronouns and their antecedents (the words that the pronouns refer back to).

(Singular   (Plural
Antecedent)   Pronoun)
For <u>a woman</u> to succeed as an umpire, <u>they</u> must overcome much prejudice.

(Singular   (Singular
Antecedent)   Pronoun)
For <u>a woman</u> to succeed as an umpire, <u>she</u> must overcome much prejudice.

The first sentence is incorrect because *a woman*, which is singular, disagrees with *they,* which is plural. (Although *they* is often used as a singular in speech, it must always be treated as a plural in writing.) The second sentence is correct because both *a woman* and *she* are singular and therefore agree.

Once again, indefinite pronouns can create agreement problems.

(Singular   (Plural
Antecedent)   Pronoun)
<u>Everyone</u> on the men's soccer team should be proud of <u>themselves</u>.

(Singular   (Singular
Antecedent)   Pronoun)
<u>Everyone</u> on the men's soccer team should be proud of <u>himself</u>.

The first sentence is incorrect because *everyone*, which is singular, disagrees with *themselves*, which is plural. The second sentence is correct because both *everyone* and *himself* are singular and therefore agree. Of course, an even better revision would simply delete the last two words, in keeping with the "less is more" principle.

Let's consider one more aspect of agreement, using this sentence as a starting point:

(Singular   (Plural
Antecedent)   Pronoun)
<u>Everybody</u> should mind <u>their</u> own business.

Clearly, there's disagreement between *Everybody*, which is singular, and *their*, which is plural, even though this is how the sentence would probably be worded in speech. But writing is more formal than speech, so the problem must be corrected. There are two ways to do so: Either the pronoun and its antecedent can both be singular, or both can be plural. Here are two singular versions:

(Singular   (Singular
Antecedent)   Pronoun)
<u>Everybody</u> should mind <u>his</u> own business.

This sentence is correct, but is guilty of gender bias.

(Singular   (Singular
Antecedent)   Pronoun)
<u>Everybody</u> should mind <u>his or her</u> own business.

Better.

Here are two plural versions:

(Plural   (Plural
Antecedent)   Pronoun)
<u>People</u> should mind <u>their</u> own business.

(Plural   (Plural
Antecedent)   Pronoun)
<u>We</u> should all mind <u>our</u> own business.

The plural approach is almost always best of all, because it avoids gender-bias without resorting to the wordy *his or her* phrasing.

ABOUT THE AUTHOR

George J. Searles is a Professor of English and Latin at Mohawk Valley Community College. He has also taught at Green Haven State Prison, on the graduate level for New School University, and on Pratt Institute's upstate campus at the Munson-Williams-Proctor Arts Institute. He has served on the governing boards of both the Modern Language Association and the North East Modern Language Association, presenting scholarly papers at the annual conventions of those and other such professional organizations. In addition, he has served as a communications consultant to many corporate clients and social services agencies, as well as the National Endowment for the Humanities and the National Science Foundation. Along with numerous articles, reviews, and poems in popular and academic periodicals, he has published three volumes of literary criticism from university presses and seven editions of *Workplace Communications: The Basics,* a textbook used on over 250 campuses here and abroad. The recipient of two SUNY Chancellor's medals for excellence, he was formerly the Carnegie Foundation "New York State Professor of the Year" and the New York State United Teachers "Higher Education Member of the Year."

INDEX

CPSIA information can be obtained
at www.ICGtesting.com
Printed in the USA
LVOW02s0325250417
532065LV00004B/8/P